# THE ESSENTIAL
# CANNING
# COOKBOOK

*For lovers of all things low, slow, simple, and old-fashioned*

Cider Mill Press Book Publishers
"Where good books are ready for press"
501 Nelson Place
Nashville, Tennessee 37214, USA

cidermillpress.com

Without limiting the exclusive rights of any author, contributor or the publisher of this publication, any unauthorized use of this publication to train generative artificial intelligence (AI) technologies is expressly prohibited. HarperCollins also exercise their rights under Article 4(3) of the Digital Single Market Directive 2019/790 and expressly reserve this publication from the text and data mining exception.

HarperCollins Publishers, Macken House, 39/40 Mayor Street Upper, Dublin 1, D01 C9W8, Ireland (https://www.harpercollins.com)

Typography: Adobe Caslon Pro, Georgia, Gotham

Image Credits: Blackberry preserves image (cover, page 31), pickled bell pepper image (cover, page 83), and images on pages 87, 103, 111, 135, 159, 171, 173, and 177 used under official license from StockFood.com. Image on page 91 courtesy of Cider Mill Press Book Publishers LLC. All other images used under official license from Adobe Stock, Pexels, Shutterstock, and Unsplash.

Printed in Canada

25 26 27 28 29 TC 5 4 3 2 1
First Edition

*Disclaimer: The recipes in this book have been carefully tested. To the best of our knowledge, they are safe for ordinary use and users. The author and publisher cannot be responsible for any hazards, loss, or damage that may occur as a result of any recipe or equipment use.*

# THE ESSENTIAL
# CANNING
# COOKBOOK

## WATER BATH & PRESSURE CANNING
## RECIPES FOR EVERY SEASON

MOLLY BRAVO

CIDER MILL PRESS

BOOK PUBLISHERS

# CONTENTS

*Introduction: Slow Living, Lasting Traditions*                         6

## PART 1: FOUNDATIONS AND TECHNIQUES                         9

Chapter 1: Getting Started                                           10

Chapter 2: Safety and Science                                        22

Chapter 3: Water Bath Canning                                        28

Chapter 4: Pressure Canning                                          40

## PART 2: ESSENTIAL RECIPES                         57

Chapter 5: Fruit                                                     58

Chapter 6: Vegetables                                                78

Chapter 7: Sauces and Chutneys                                      114

Chapter 8: Broths, Stocks, and Soups                                138

Chapter 9: One-Jar Meals                                            168

Chapter 10: Desserts in Jars                                        188

*Reference Charts*                                                  198

*Index*                                                             201

*Bibliography*                                                      206

*Acknowledgments*                                                   206

*About the Author*                                                  207

# SLOW LIVING, LASTING TRADITIONS

Twenty years in professional kitchens taught me how to move fast, push harder, do more. But it was a weathered box of recipe cards that taught me how to slow down.

I found them on my mother's counter, where they'd sat for 43 years—my grandmother Alberta's precise handwriting detailing everything from tomato sauce to peach preserves. Between the cooking-stained cards and careful notes, I found something more valuable than recipes. I received clarity about how I want to design my life and the steps I'm going to take to get there. And hence, my personal journey toward slow living took shape.

I'm not a homesteading expert or a back-to-the-land guru. I'm a chef, mother, and entrepreneur who spent two decades in the relentless pace of professional kitchens before realizing I was chasing the wrong dream. My real dream? It's simpler—and harder. I want to live off the land as much as possible. I want to homeschool my son, teaching him that real wealth isn't measured in dollars but in the freedom to do what lights you up and to be present for the people who mean the most to you. I want slow Sundays with dirt under my fingernails and lazy midweek mornings where I can sip a cup of coffee and watch the sunrise.

Surrounded by modern gadgets in my commercial kitchen, I realized that all my technical expertise had somehow disconnected me from the simple wisdom that kept our ancestors fed and communities connected through countless seasons.

This yearning for simplicity is something many of us experience. It's a recognition that our rush toward convenience has come at a great cost. We've traded food security for instant gratification, genuine connection for digital interaction, and generational knowledge for Google searches.

I see this same hunger reflected in others: young parents wanting to feed their children without plastic, urban professionals seeking something real in an increasingly artificial world, retirees recalling the rhythm of snapping beans with their grandmothers …

Quality of life, for me, means having time—time to explore, to create, to work the soil, to teach my son what it means to truly appreciate what we have. You can't find that kind of time in a convenience culture that constantly pushes for more, faster, easier. But you can create it, one jar of preserves at a time. My grandmother Alberta's recipe cards showed me how. Beyond the instructions for timing and temperatures, they contained a philosophy for living:

*Start early on canning days; the morning air is cool, and your energy is fresh.*

*Label everything right away; the memory of what's in those jars fades quickly.*

*Share your abundance freely; extra jars are deposits in the community bank.*

*Use the right tools when you can, but remember:*
*My grandparents preserved entire harvests with just a pot and some jars.*

Many of us are choosing to step away from the hustle and toward something more intentional. Each recipe, each technique, each bit of preserved wisdom is a small act of rebellion against a system that wants us to be dependent on industrial food and industrial schedules. Whether you have an hour or a day, this book will help you reclaim the lost art of food preservation. More importantly, it will help you reclaim your time, connecting you to the natural rhythms of the seasons and the satisfaction of providing for yourself and your family.

This book serves as a bridge between old wisdom and modern needs. You won't find complicated equipment lists or intimidating techniques. Instead, you'll discover how your great-grandmother's methods of food preservation remain relevant today. Whether you're preserving your garden's bounty or maximizing farmers market finds, these pages will guide you through canning methods that would make our ancestors proud.

As you embark on this journey, remember that every expert was once a beginner. Every grandmother who mastered canning started with her first jar. The most important step is to begin where you are, with what you have, and let your skills grow naturally.

Just as generations of home canners have done before us, we'll start by understanding where we've been so we can better appreciate where we're going.

PART 1

# FOUNDATIONS AND TECHNIQUES

Chapter 1: Getting Started      10

Chapter 2: Safety and Science      22

Chapter 3: Water Bath Canning      28

Chapter 4: Pressure Canning      40

CHAPTER 1

GETTING
STARTED

## THE WORLD OF FOOD PRESERVATION

Long before pressure canners or mason jars, our ancestors devised ingenious ways to keep food edible through lean times. Every culture had its methods, its wisdom born of necessity and refined through generations of careful observation.

Although our ancestors were drying and fermenting foods for millennia, canning as we know it emerged around 1795, initiated by Napoleon's need to feed his armies. Chef Nicolas Appert discovered that sealing food in glass bottles and heating them properly prevented spoilage. He won a government prize for his discovery in 1810, forever changing food preservation.

Appert was a culinary professional who spent 14 years perfecting his technique. The technology spread quickly. By 1813, England had its first commercial canning factory, and by 1825, Americans were selling canned oysters, fruits, meats, and vegetables in New York. During the Great Depression, community canning centers emerged, where people shared equipment and knowledge to ensure their neighbors had enough food.

During World War II, growing victory gardens and using home canning became acts of patriotism. In 1943 alone, Americans canned more than 4 billion jars of food. This history proves our capacity for resilience and community care. By learning to preserve our food, we're continuing a tradition of knowledge-sharing that has helped communities survive countless challenges.

In the pages ahead, we'll explore both the science and art of food preservation. We'll learn the rules that keep us safe and the techniques that ensure our food remains delicious. Most importantly, we'll reconnect with a tradition of taking care of ourselves and one another, just as our ancestors did. As my grandmother used to say, a full pantry is better than a full wallet.

## BUILDING CONFIDENCE AS A BEGINNER

If the thought of canning makes you a little nervous, you're not alone. Plenty of beginners worry about messing up a batch, getting the seal right, or—let's be honest—botulism (see page 12). The idea of putting food into jars that will sit on a shelf for months might feel intimidating at first. I want to reassure you that canning is completely safe when you follow a few simple, time-tested steps. I promise, those steps are easier than you think.

**Step 1.** Confident canning is understanding that there are two main methods: water bath canning and pressure canning. Water bath canning is used for high-acid foods like fruits, jams, and pickles, while pressure canning is necessary for low-acid foods like vegetables, meats, and soups. Knowing which method to use is the key to safe, successful preservation.

**Step 2.** Keep your workspace clean and organized. A tidy setup not only makes the process easier, but also helps prevent contamination. Before you get started, wash your jars, lids, and tools, and make sure everything is ready to go.

**Step 3.** Start with trusted recipes from reputable sources, like the USDA Complete Guide to Home Canning, to build a solid foundation in safe canning techniques. Every tested recipe is carefully designed to keep your food safe and shelf-stable, so resist the urge to tweak ingredient amounts or skip steps—no matter how minor they seem. By following time-honored methods from the start, you're mastering the craft the right way.

**Step 4.** After your jars have been processed and cooled, check the seals. A properly sealed jar means your food is safely preserved and ready for long-term storage. The lid should be concave and shouldn't flex when pressed. This is your sign that the vacuum seal is holding strong.

The best way to get comfortable with canning? Just start. Every experienced canner once stood right where you are—feeling unsure, second-guessing, and probably overthinking the whole thing. But the only way to get past that discomfort is to get a few jars under your belt. Ease in with a simple jam (see page 38 for a strawberry jam recipe for beginners) or a batch of canned vegetables (see page 54 for a green beans recipe for beginners). Once you see how easy and satisfying canning can be, you'll wonder why you didn't start sooner!

Trust the process, take it one step at a time, and before you know it, canning will feel like second nature.

> ## THE ROLE OF pH IN BOTULISM PREVENTION
>
> Let's talk about botulism for a second because I know it's a big fear. It only thrives in low-acid, oxygen-free environments, which is why low-acid foods like meats and vegetables need pressure canning. If you follow a tested recipe and process your jars correctly, botulism isn't a concern. High-acid foods like jams, pickles, and tomatoes with added acidity are naturally safe for water bath canning, and pressure canning ensures that low-acid foods reach the right temperatures to destroy harmful bacteria. When you use the correct method, your preserves will be safe, shelf-stable, and delicious.

## SETTING UP YOUR CANNING KITCHEN

Having the right tools on hand makes all the difference in home canning. The proper equipment not only creates a quicker and easier process, but also ensures that your preserves are safe and shelf-stable.

Getting started doesn't have to be expensive or overwhelming. Many of the essentials are budget friendly, and if you keep an eye out, you can often find jars, canners, and tools at thrift stores or yard sales, or you could even borrow them from friends and family.

You don't need a fancy, high-tech setup to start canning—just the basics. Once you get comfortable with the process, invest in extra tools that streamline your workflow and save time. For now, focus on what matters most: having the right foundational tools to help you work efficiently, to avoid common mistakes, and to ensure that every jar you seal is safe and ready for long-term storage.

Since this book is designed for absolute beginners, I've put together a comprehensive list of everything you'll need, including the most basic kitchen tools. I also explain why each item is important, so you'll know exactly what you need—and what you don't—to get started confidently.

## CANNING EQUIPMENT

**Boiling water bath canner (or large stockpot with a canning rack):** For processing high-acid foods like jams, pickles, and tomatoes. It must be deep enough to fully submerge jars with at least 1 to 2 inches of water covering the lids.

**Pressure canner:** A must-have for safely preserving low-acid foods like vegetables, meats, and soups. Unlike a regular pressure cooker, a true pressure canner is designed to maintain the high temperatures necessary to eliminate harmful bacteria. Choose between a dial-gauge pressure canner, which requires periodic calibration, or a weighted-gauge pressure canner, which is easier to maintain but offers fewer pressure adjustments.

**Canning rack:** For keeping jars elevated inside the pot (preventing direct contact with the bottom, which causes breakage). If you don't have one, a round cake rack or a layer of extra jar rings works in a pinch.

**Mason jars with lids and bands:** For safely containing preserves. Bands can be reused, but always use new lids for every batch to ensure a proper seal.

**Jar lifter:** For safely lifting hot jars in and out of boiling water.

**Canning funnel:** For filling jars neatly while maintaining proper headspace (the space between the food and the lid).

**Bubble remover/headspace tool (or chopstick):** For removing trapped air bubbles inside jars and helping to measure correct headspace.

**Kitchen timer:** For tracking precise processing times, which is critical for food safety.

## CHOOSING THE RIGHT JARS

There are many brands of canning jars available. The most important thing is to use jars that come with both a lid and a screw band. These two-piece lids are essential for creating a vacuum seal, which ensures your food stays safe and shelf-stable. Two well-known and trusted brands in the United States are Ball and Kerr, both of which have been used by home canners for generations.

However, there are other jars on the market, including store-brand and imported options. As long as the jars are designed for home canning and use standard two-piece lids, they should work.

## STANDARD JAR SIZES AND THEIR USES

Canning jars come in a variety of sizes, but the following are the most common.

**Half-pint (8 oz):** Perfect for jams, jellies, and sauces.

**Pint (16 oz):** A versatile size used for fruits, vegetables, salsas, and sauces.

**Quart (32 oz):** Great for whole fruits, large batches of tomatoes, and soups.

**Half-gallon (64 oz):** Typically used for pickling and fermenting, but not recommended for canning low-acid foods.

Most jars come in both regular-mouth and wide-mouth varieties. Regular-mouth jars have a smaller opening and are best for liquids, jams, and sauces. Wide-mouth jars have a larger opening, making them easier to fill with whole fruits and vegetables. If you're just starting out, look for canning jar sets that include jars, new lids, and bands together. If you're reusing jars from previous batches, make sure to inspect them before using and discard any with cracks, chips, or rusted bands.

Start with the essentials, then add equipment as your skills grow. Prioritize safety and durability, and remember: Great canning doesn't require expensive tools, just the right ones!

## WHY YOU NEED NEW LIDS EACH TIME

The flat metal lid on a canning jar has a special sealing compound that softens during processing, creating an airtight seal as the jar cools. But here's the important part: This compound only works once. Once a lid has been used, it may not seal properly again, which could lead to spoilage or food-safety issues, so always use a fresh lid for every batch. The screw bands, however, are reusable. Their only job is to hold the lid in place during processing. Once your jars are sealed, take the bands off for storage and use them again for your next canning session.

## CHOOSING THE BEST PRODUCE FOR CANNING

Canning is all about capturing the best flavors of the season, but the final product is only as good as the ingredients you start with. That means if you start with bland, overripe, or bruised produce, your preserves will reflect that. The key to high-quality canned goods is starting with produce that's fresh, at peak ripeness, and free from damage. No technique fixes poor ingredients.

It might be tempting to think, *This fruit is a little past its prime. I'll just can it instead of throwing it out.* Remember: Canning doesn't improve quality; it preserves what's already there. Overripe fruits break down faster, leading to mushy textures and displeasing flavors. More importantly, canning does not kill spoilage bacteria. The best rule of thumb? If you wouldn't eat it fresh, don't can it.

When selecting produce, look for firm, ripe, and unblemished fruits and vegetables. Tomatoes should be deep red, slightly firm, and fragrant—not streaked with green (underripe) or mushy (overripe). Peaches and pears should give just slightly when pressed but not be too soft. Cucumbers for pickling should be crisp, with no yellow spots (a sign of over-ripeness). Green beans should snap cleanly when bent, and corn kernels should be plump and release a milky liquid when pierced.

## HANDLING AND STORING PRODUCE PROPERLY

How you store fresh produce before preserving is just as important as how you can it. Not all fruits and vegetables should be stored the same way, and handling them correctly helps slow spoilage while maintaining quality.

Some produce, such as berries, leafy greens, and soft fruits (peaches, plums), should be kept in the refrigerator so they stay fresh longer. On the other hand, tomatoes, onions, garlic, potatoes, and squash should never be refrigerated, as cold temperatures alter their texture and flavor. Storing these items in a cool, dry place helps them last longer and retain their natural taste.

It's also best to hold off on washing produce until you're ready to use it. Moisture speeds up spoilage, especially for delicate foods like berries and soft fruits. Keeping them dry and rinsing just before processing ensures they stay fresh for as long as possible. Additionally,

### SHOP SMARTER FOR THE BEST QUALITY AND PRICES

The best preserves start with the freshest ingredients, and a farmers market is one of the best places to find just-picked produce, often harvested only hours before it reaches the stand. If you're looking for the widest selection, shop early in the day, before popular items sell out. But if your goal is to save money, consider shopping right before closing, when some vendors discount leftover produce rather than take it home.

Buying in bulk during peak season is another great way to save money while getting the best quality. When fruits and vegetables are at their most abundant, prices drop, making it the perfect time to stock up. If you plan ahead, using my seasonal availability guide (see page 18), you'll be in a position to take advantage of these lower prices and preserve food at its freshest. Another budget-friendly option is purchasing "seconds," which are slightly imperfect or misshapen produce often sold at a discount. These work just as well for jams, sauces, and salsas, where appearance doesn't matter as much as flavor.

If you want a steady supply of local produce, consider joining a Community Supported Agriculture (CSA) program or a community garden, both of which offer fresh, seasonal food at a lower cost while supporting farmers. If you grow your own produce, swapping with like-minded neighbors is a great way to add variety to your pantry without spending extra money.

handling produce with care is key. Bruising leads to early decay, so take extra caution when transporting and storing delicate items.

## PRESERVING WITH THE SEASONS

A little planning goes a long way when it comes to canning. The best time to start is as soon as crops begin ripening, whether you're harvesting from your own garden or keeping an eye on what's showing up at the farmers market.

With a little strategy, canning becomes more efficient, less overwhelming, and—most importantly—a whole lot more enjoyable.

## SETTING YOURSELF UP FOR SUCCESS

A successful canning season begins long before the first jar is filled. One of the best ways to prepare is by thinking about what you and your family actually eat. Assessing your household's eating habits will help you determine not just what you eat, but how much.

Once you have a clear idea of what you want to can, take stock of your storage space. Even if you plan to preserve a variety of foods, there's only so much room in a pantry or basement for jars. Consider whether you have shelves, bins, or cabinets available and if you need additional storage solutions. Some foods may be better suited for freezing or dehydration, both of which can stretch

## GET TO KNOW YOUR HARDINESS ZONE

Home canning allows you to plan ahead and make the most of each season's bounty. Whether you're aiming for a pantry stocked with essentials or simply want to enjoy your favorite summer flavors year-round, successful canning requires a bit of foresight. Without a plan, you may find yourself overwhelmed by a sudden influx of ripe produce, short on storage space, or scrambling to find the right equipment at the last minute. Anticipating when produce is in season in your area and taking the time to think ahead will allow you to work efficiently, reduce waste, and enjoy the process without stress.

The produce guide in this book is based on USDA Plant Hardiness Zones 4 to 7, which cover a large portion of the United States, including much of the Midwest and Northeast and parts of the Pacific Northwest. If you live in a warmer or colder climate, you may need to adjust your timeline accordingly. If you're unsure what's in season in your area, here are a few great resources to help:

- Your state's cooperative extension website: Most university-run extension programs offer seasonal availability charts and food preservation guides.

- Online tools like **seasonalfoodguide.org**: Provides state-by-state seasonal availability.

- Farmers markets: Talking to local growers is one of the best ways to find out what's coming when.

your storage capacity. Having a realistic view of your available space will prevent you from overcanning and will help you focus on the most useful and space-efficient foods.

## TIMING AND BATCHING

The key to making canning manageable is to break it into smaller, planned sessions rather than attempting to process everything at once. Each season offers different preservation opportunities, so aligning your canning schedule with peak harvest times ensures you are preserving food at its best.

Batch processing is another way to streamline canning days. Grouping foods by preservation method makes the process smoother; focus on high-acid foods like jams and pickles one day and tackle low-acid foods like vegetables and meats on another day. Some foods lend themselves to a multistep approach. For example, when pressure-canning tomato sauce, consider simultaneously dehydrating the tomato skins to make tomato powder. Finding ways to integrate multiple preservation methods helps make the most of your harvest while maximizing efficiency.

Keeping a canning journal is also a helpful tool for planning. Writing down what you preserved, how much you made, and any recipe notes will help guide your decisions for the following season. Tracking your canning efforts ensures you're preserving food in a way that best meets your needs.

# A MONTH-BY-MONTH CANNING GUIDE TO SEASONAL PRODUCE

By following nature's rhythm, you can build a pantry that's stocked with peak-season flavors all year long—without feeling rushed or overwhelmed. Here's a month-by-month breakdown of what's in season and how best to preserve it.

## MARCH

**Asparagus:** Freeze or pickle.

**Rhubarb:** Freeze, candy, or make jam.

**Spinach:** Freeze or dehydrate.

## APRIL

**Mustard greens:** Freeze or dehydrate.

**Strawberries:** Make jam, freeze, or can as syrup.

**Swiss chard:** Blanch and freeze for later use.

## MAY

**Berries (various):** Make jam, freeze, or dehydrate.

**Peas:** Freeze or pressure-can.

**Radishes:** Pickle or ferment.

## JUNE

**Cherries:** Make jam, freeze, or can in syrup.

**Tomatoes:** Can into sauces or salsas, or pressure-can whole.

**Zucchini:** Freeze, dehydrate, or pickle.

## JULY

**Cucumbers:** Pickle, using water bath canning.

**Peaches:** Make jam, can in syrup, or freeze slices.

**Peppers (bell, hot, etc.):** Freeze, dehydrate, or pickle.

## AUGUST

**Corn:** Freeze, can as soup, or dehydrate.

**Melons:** Freeze for smoothies or make fruit syrup.

**Tomatoes:** Continue preserving through canning or freezing.

## SEPTEMBER

**Apples:** Make applesauce or butter or dehydrate slices.

**Pears:** Make jam, can in syrup, or dehydrate.

**Pumpkins:** Pressure-can purée or dehydrate for powder.

## OCTOBER

**Beets:** Pickle, pressure-can, or store in a root cellar.

**Carrots:** Pressure-can, freeze, or dehydrate.

**Squash (winter varieties):** Freeze purée or store whole in a cool, dry place.

## NOVEMBER TO FEBRUARY

**Cranberries:** Make sauce, can in syrup, or dehydrate.

**Garlic:** Store in a cool, dry, well-ventilated space.

**Onions:** Store in mesh bags or dehydrate for powder.

**Potatoes:** Pressure-can or store in a root cellar.

**Sweet potatoes:** Store at room temperature to cure or freeze mashed.

## SMART STORAGE

It's important to make sure your jars are properly sealed, but it's equally as important to store them correctly. Once your jars have cooled and sealed, what's next? Where you store them, how you track them, and how you check for spoilage are just as important as the canning process itself.

Proper storage extends the shelf life of your preserves and helps you stay organized, so nothing gets lost or forgotten. Even properly sealed jars can be compromised by poor storage conditions. Here are my six best practices for safe and smart storage.

1. **Label and date everything.** It's easy to lose track of when a jar was processed, so always write the contents and date on the lid or jar label.

2. **Store in a cool, dark place.** Avoid direct sunlight. Light causes color and texture changes, and over time it degrades nutrients in canned foods. The best storage temperature is 50°F to 70°F. Avoid places that are too warm. Never store jars near stoves, radiators, or water heaters, where heat can weaken the seal. Extreme heat or freezing temperatures break down the quality of food and weaken seals.

3. **Prevent moisture exposure.** Rusty lids lead to broken seals, so store jars in a dry area. If you live in a humid climate, check regularly for moisture buildup.

4. **Don't stack jars.** While it might be tempting to stack jars to save space, the USDA advises against it because stacking creates pressure on the seals, leading to seal failure over time. If you must stack, place a sturdy piece of cardboard between layers to reduce the pressure.

5. **Check seals regularly.** Every month, take a quick look at your jars. If any lids are bulging or leaking or have come loose, discard them immediately.

6. **Use the oldest preserves first.** Follow the First In, First Out (FIFO) rule by placing the oldest jars in the front and newer jars in the back.

## TYPICAL SHELF LIFE OF HOME-CANNED FOODS

The USDA recommends using home-canned goods within one year for the best quality, but properly stored jars can last longer. The key is knowing when food is still safe versus when it's past its prime.

| FOOD TYPE | SHELF LIFE (BEST QUALITY) |
|---|---|
| Water bath canned foods | Up to 18 months (Best within 1 year) |
| Pressure canned vegetables and meats | 2 to 5 years (Best within 2 years) |
| Pickled foods | 1 year (Best texture within 6 to 12 months) |
| Jams and jellies | 1 to 2 years (Sugar helps extend freshness) |

## SIGNS OF SPOILAGE: WHEN IN DOUBT, THROW IT OUT

Even if a jar looks fine, always check for signs of spoilage before consuming. Never taste home-canned food unless you're 100% sure it's safe. Botulism, one of the most dangerous foodborne illnesses, has no smell, taste, or visible signs (see page 12).

### WHAT TO LOOK FOR BEFORE OPENING

**Bulging or domed lids.** This means gas has built up inside, a sign of bacterial growth. Discard the jar contents immediately.

**Leaks or broken seals.** If liquid has leaked out or the seal has popped, discard the jar contents immediately.

**Mold or discoloration.** If you see fuzzy growth or dark spots inside the jar, don't take any chances. Discard the jar contents immediately.

**Fizzing or spurting liquid.** If the liquid foams or bubbles out when you open the jar, that's a sign of bacterial activity. Discard the jar contents immediately.

**Unpleasant or off smell.** Good canned food should smell fresh. If something smells sour, musty, or just off, it's not worth the risk. Discard the jar contents immediately.

**Slimy or mushy texture.** If the food feels slimy or unusually soft, bacteria may have started breaking it down. Discard the jar contents immediately.

If you notice any of these signs, discard the food immediately—do not taste it! When in doubt, throw it out.

## TROUBLESHOOTING COMMON STORAGE ISSUES

Even if you follow best practices, small issues can still arise. Here's how to handle them.

**Cloudy brine in pickles?** Hard water or table salt (which contains additives) causes cloudy liquid. Use canning salt or distilled water to prevent this.

**Mold on lids?** Food residue on jar rims allows mold to grow under the lid. Always wipe rims clean before sealing and check for proper headspace.

**Rusty lids?** Storing jars in a humid or damp environment causes lids to rust. To prevent this, remove the bands after jars have sealed and store jars in a dry area.

CHAPTER 2

# SAFETY AND SCIENCE

Canning is a simple, time-tested way to preserve food, but like anything worth doing, it's important to do it the correct way. When you understand the process and follow a few key safety principles, you'll end up with jars that seal properly, food that stays safe to eat, and a pantry stocked with homemade preserves you feel good about.

Water bath canning is the go-to method for preserving high-acid foods like jams, jellies, fruits, pickles, and tomatoes with added acid. The process is simple: Filled jars are submerged in boiling water, reaching 212°F, and held there for a set amount of time. This heat kills bacteria, yeasts, and molds while driving out air, allowing the lids to seal as the jars cool. The natural acidity of the food, combined with the heat from processing, creates an environment where botulism spores can't survive, making this method both effective and safe for long-term storage.

Pressure canning is a game changer when it comes to safely preserving low-acid foods like vegetables, meats, poultry, soups, and broths. Unlike water bath canning, which relies on acidity to keep bacteria at bay, pressure canning harnesses high heat and steam to do the job. Inside a sealed pressure canner, temperatures climb to 240°F to 250°F, hot enough to destroy botulism spores that could otherwise survive in a low-acid, oxygen-free environment. Without that level of heat, harmful bacteria multiplies undetected, which is why following proper processing methods is so crucial.

When it comes to food safety, there are no shortcuts. Stick with tested, science-backed methods, and you'll have preserved foods that are both safe and packed with flavor.

## HOW CANNING WORKS: THE BASICS

At its core, canning is about using heat to kill microorganisms, sealing food in an airtight jar, and preventing spoilage. There are two key parts to this process:

1. Heating the food in jars to destroy bacteria, yeasts, and molds that cause spoilage
2. Creating a vacuum seal as the jar cools, preventing new bacteria from getting in

When you submerge a jar of food in boiling water (for high-acid foods) or process it under high pressure and steam (for low-acid foods), you're raising the temperature high enough to destroy harmful microorganisms. As the jar cools, the air inside contracts, pulling the lid down and forming a vacuum seal. This is what makes canned food shelf-stable.

One of the most important safety rules in canning is matching the correct processing method to the food's acidity level. High-acid foods—tomatoes, apples, peaches, pears, berries—are safe for water bath canning because the acid naturally prevents the growth of dangerous bacteria. Low-acid foods—beans, peas, carrots, corn, potatoes—must be pressure canned to reach high enough temperatures to kill botulism spores, which thrive in low-acid, oxygen-free environments, like a sealed jar. Boiling water only reaches 212°F, which isn't hot enough to kill them. A pressure canner, however, reaches 240°F to 250°F, which destroys them completely.

If something goes wrong—if the food isn't heated properly, if the jar doesn't seal, or if the recipe isn't followed exactly—the risk of spoilage increases. That's why understanding acidity, processing times, and recipe safety is so important. If you're unsure about a food's acidity, use pH strips or a digital pH meter to test it.

## KEY INGREDIENTS FOR SAFE AND SUCCESSFUL CANNING

Canning is both a science and an art, and certain ingredients play a crucial role in preserving food safely and maintaining texture, flavor, and shelf life. While some of these ingredients may seem optional in everyday cooking, they are nonnegotiable in canning because they affect acidity, stability, and food safety. Here, I break down the essential ingredients and explain why they matter, how they work, and how to use them properly.

### 1. ACIDITY: THE KEY TO FOOD SAFETY

One of the most important elements in canning is acidity, which helps prevent the growth of harmful bacteria like *Clostridium botulinum*, the toxin responsible for botulism. Acidity plays a crucial role in water bath canning, as high-acid foods (pH 4.6 or lower) naturally prevent bacterial growth. If a food isn't acidic enough, its acidity can be safely increased by adding specific quantities of vinegar, lemon juice, or citric acid.

**WHY FOLLOWING TESTED RECIPES IS NONNEGOTIABLE**

Canning is a precise science, and every tested recipe has been designed for safety, so now is not the time to experiment with ingredient swaps. Altering a tested recipe can lead to unsafe results. Stick to trusted sources, and if you have any questions, cross-reference the recipe with the USDA. Remember:

1. Acidity levels are carefully balanced. Changing vinegar or lemon juice types alters the pH, making food unsafe.

2. Processing times are precise. They ensure heat penetrates the entire jar. Changing jar sizes or food density affects heat flow.

3. Ingredient substitutions can be risky. For example, swapping fresh tomatoes for canned in salsa changes the acidity enough to require pressure canning.

If you want to customize recipes, only modify within safe guidelines. Adjusting spices is fine, but altering acid or sugar levels is not.

**Vinegar (5% acidity):** Used in pickles, relishes, and chutneys, vinegar must have at least 5% acidity to ensure safe preservation, so always check the label. Never dilute vinegar or substitute homemade vinegar, as its acidity level may be inconsistent.

**Lemon juice:** Often added to tomatoes and fruit preserves to ensure proper acidity. Always use bottled lemon juice for canning, as fresh lemons vary in acidity.

**Citric acid:** A dry, shelf-stable alternative to lemon juice, commonly used in canning tomatoes.

If a recipe calls for vinegar, lemon juice, or citric acid, it's not just for flavor—it's there to keep your food safe. Do not reduce or substitute acid levels in tested recipes.

## 2. SUGAR: MORE THAN JUST SWEETNESS

**Sugar is essential in jams, jellies, and fruit preserves, but it does more than just sweeten:** 1) It helps preserve color and texture by slowing oxidation; 2) It extends shelf life by binding with water, making it unavailable for mold and bacteria growth; and 3) It aids in gel formation when used with pectin in jams and jellies. There are different types of sugar to consider.

**Granulated white sugar:** Most commonly used for canning, as it dissolves easily and doesn't affect acidity.

**Brown sugar and honey:** Occasionally used, but they contain more moisture and may affect texture and shelf stability, so only use if a recipe from a trusted source specifically calls for them.

**Low-sugar or no-sugar pectin options:** Not sugar but allowed for reduced-sugar preserves. Must only be used in recipes that specifically call for them.

Reducing sugar in a standard recipe can cause jams and jellies to fail, leading to spoilage, so if you are looking for a low-sugar option, choose a well-known low-sugar pectin product.

## 3. SALT: ESSENTIAL FOR PICKLING

**Salt is crucial in pickling because:** 1) It controls microbial growth. Proper salt concentration helps prevent spoilage; 2) It enhances texture, drawing out moisture and keeping pickles crisp; and 3) It balances flavor. Without salt, pickles may taste dull. Not all salts are created equal!

**Pickling salt (canning salt):** The best choice for canning, as it is pure salt with no additives that could cloud the brine.

**Table salt:** Contains anticaking agents and iodine, which can cause discoloration and cloudy brine. Not recommended for use in canning.

**Kosher salt:** Can be used if it's pure salt, but the flake size varies, so measure by weight instead of volume. (This means weighing the pickling salt called for in a recipe and substituting the same weight of kosher salt.)

**Sea salt:** Can be used, but check the label to make sure it's free of additives.

If a tested pickling recipe calls for a specific salt measurement, do not reduce it. This could affect the food safety and texture.

## 4. PECTIN: THE SCIENCE BEHIND JAMS AND JELLIES

Pectin is a natural carbohydrate found in fruits that helps jams and jellies set. Some fruits, like apples and citrus peels, are naturally high in pectin, while others, like strawberries and peaches, need added pectin to achieve the right consistency.

There are different types of pectin, and it's important to use the correct type for your recipe.

**Regular pectin:** Requires a high amount of sugar to activate the gelling process. Best for traditional jams and jellies.

**Low-sugar or no-sugar pectin:** Designed for making jams with less or no sugar. If you're reducing sugar, you must use this type of pectin.

**Liquid pectin:** Comes predissolved and cannot be used interchangeably with powdered pectin.

**Natural pectin sources:** Pectin is naturally high in some fruits, such as apples, quinces, and citrus peels, which can be used to naturally thicken jams.

Using the wrong pectin—or skipping it alto-gether—can result in runny jams or overly stiff preserves. If a recipe calls for a specific pectin type, stick with it to ensure the best results.

## 5. WATER: THE UNSUNG HERO OF CANNING

It may seem simple, but the water you use can impact your canning results. Hard water, which contains minerals like calcium and magnesium, can cause cloudy brine in pickles, darkened preserves in fruit canning, and residue on jars after processing. Use filtered or distilled water for pickling and canning delicate fruits. If using hard water, add 1 tablespoon of white vinegar per gallon of water you put in your canning pot to help prevent residue buildup.

---

### CANNING IS SAFE WHEN YOU FOLLOW THE SCIENCE

Home canning is a simple, time-tested process, and when you follow the basic rules—tested recipes, proper processing methods, and safety checks—you'll have a pantry stocked with safe, delicious food.

Always do the following:

1. Stick to tested recipes from trusted sources to ensure safe, high-quality results.

2. Use the exact ingredients specified in the recipe; do not substitute any ingredient unless recommended in the recipe.

3. Maintain correct acidity by using the quantity and type of acid called for in the recipe. This is nonnegotiable.

4. Use fresh ingredients (overripe produce can lead to spoilage).

5. Clean your produce and equipment well and never skip sanitizing your jars.

---

CHAPTER 3

WATER BATH
CANNING

Water bath canning is where many preservers start. It's a simple yet powerful method that requires little more than a large pot of boiling water, fresh produce, and clean jars. While easy to learn, it still demands attention to proper technique to ensure your food remains safe and shelf-stable.

Designed for preserving high-acid foods (pH 4.6 or lower) in jars, this method prevents bacterial growth in food by combining the power of heat with acidity. Boiling water (212°F) eliminates spoilage organisms naturally present in foods and creates a vacuum seal on jars for safe storage.

High-acid foods include:
- Fruits (apples, peaches, plums, cherries, rhubarb, grapes, berries)
- Jams, jellies, and fruit juice
- Pickles and relishes (acidified with vinegar)
- Tomatoes with added acid (lemon juice or citric acid)

## HOT PACKING VS. RAW PACKING

There are two primary methods for filling jars with foods you want to preserve: hot packing and raw packing. The way you fill your jars affects the texture, flavor, and shelf stability of your food, so it's important to understand when to use each method.

Hot packing involves briefly cooking food before placing it into jars and covering it with boiling liquid. This method is ideal for soft fruits, tomatoes with added acid, jams, jellies, and most pickles. Preheating helps food shrink slightly, which means more fits into each jar while reducing air pockets that lead to discoloration. It also improves the way food absorbs flavors, ensuring a more even, well-balanced taste. One of the biggest benefits of hot packing is that it creates better liquid coverage, preventing food from floating to the top of the jar and making for a more stable, longer-lasting preserve.

Raw packing, on the other hand, means placing uncooked food directly into jars before adding hot liquid. This method works well for firmer produce like apples, grapes, and whole peaches, as well as certain vegetables and meats that will be pressure canned. Some prefer raw packing because it saves time and retains heat-sensitive nutrients that might break down during precooking. However, because the food isn't heated beforehand, it often releases air during processing, which leads to floating or slight liquid loss.

Choosing between hot packing and raw packing depends on the type of food you're preserving and the outcome you want. If you're canning high-acid foods and want the best texture and shelf stability, hot packing is usually the way to go. If you're working with firm, moisture-rich foods or need to save time, raw packing might be a better fit. No matter which method you choose, following tested recipes ensures that your preserves are not just delicious but also safe for long-term storage.

## WATER LEVELS AND JAR PREPARATION

Before you even start filling jars, taking a few moments to set up your canning station properly makes all the difference in achieving safe, consistent results. One of the most important steps is managing your water levels. Before processing, fill your canning pot with enough water to completely cover the jars by at least 1 to 2 inches. This ensures even heat distribution and proper sealing. During processing, keep an eye on the water level. Evaporation happens faster than you might expect. If needed, carefully add boiling water to maintain full coverage, but avoid sudden temperature changes that could lead to jar breakage.

Equally important is jar preparation. Wash your jars and lids in hot, soapy water, rinsing them thoroughly to remove any lingering debris. To ensure they are sterilized and ready for use, submerge them in simmering water for about 10 minutes, keeping them hot until you're ready to fill them. This step is key to preventing thermal shock, which causes jars to crack when exposed to sudden temperature changes.

Finally, be sure to position your canning rack properly before processing. The rack elevates the jars, allowing water to circulate evenly around them, which is essential for consistent heat penetration. If you don't have a traditional rack, a silicone trivet or even a layer of extra jar rings works in a pinch. A well-prepared setup not only streamlines the canning process, but also ensures your preserves remain safe and shelf-stable.

## TIME AND TEMPERATURE

When I first started canning, I ruined an entire batch of tomato sauce simply because I let the water temperature drop too low. That one mistake taught me something every canner needs to understand: Time and temperature control everything.

For high-acid foods like fruits, pickles, and tomatoes with added acid, processing must happen in a boiling water bath at 212°F. This combination of heat and acidity is what makes these preserves safe for long-term storage. But hitting the right temperature isn't enough; you also must time it correctly. Start counting the processing time only once the water reaches a full rolling boil and the jars are fully submerged by at least 1 to 2 inches. Starting the count too soon results in underprocessed food, which may spoil on the shelf.

After processing, cooling the jars properly is just as important. Let jars cool naturally on a towel-lined surface, undisturbed. Avoid placing jars in an ice bath or anywhere with a cold draft, as rapid temperature changes can weaken the seal or even crack the jars. Once cooled, check each lid by pressing gently on the center. It should be concave and not flex under pressure. While the satisfying "ping" of a sealing lid is a good sign, it's not a guarantee; always double-check the seals after 12 to 24 hours.

Consistency is key when it comes to processing, so here a few best practices: If you're using the hot-pack method, make sure your food is still bubbling hot when you ladle it into jars. If you're raw packing, always start with room-temperature ingredients. Never pull cold produce straight from the fridge, as it throws off processing times. Keep additional hot water simmering on the stove, in case you need to top off the water in the canning pot. A good kitchen thermometer is a must; guesswork has no place in canning. And, of course, always follow the recommended processing times for your specific recipe, as variations in jar size and food density impact how long it takes to reach a safe internal temperature.

Mastering time and temperature takes practice, but once you do, you'll never have to second-guess whether your preserves are safe. Stick to the process, trust your tools, and resist the temptation to take shortcuts. Your future self will thank you when you open a perfect jar of homemade preserves months down the line.

### GEL SETTING: HOW TO AVOID RUNNY PRESERVES

One of the biggest surprises when you start making jam is that it often looks way too thin when you're ladling it into jars. You might be convinced you've just made a big batch of fruit syrup instead of a thick, spreadable preserve. But don't panic—this is totally normal! Jams and jellies thicken as they cool, thanks to pectin, a natural carbohydrate in fruit that works with sugar, acid, and heat to create that perfect gel. The trick is knowing how to balance these elements and how to test for doneness before you start sealing up jars.

Some fruits, like apples, citrus peels, and quinces, are naturally packed with pectin and gel easily. Others, like strawberries and peaches, need a little extra help in the form of added pectin. The right balance of sugar and acid is just as important—too little, and your jam won't set; too much heat, and you'll break down the pectin entirely, leaving you with a runny mess.

So how do you know when your jam is ready? There are a few simple tests. My favorite is the wrinkle test: Just drop a spoonful of hot jam onto a plate you've chilled in the freezer. Let it sit for a minute, then push it gently with your finger. If it wrinkles, it's ready to go. If it's still runny, it needs more time on the stove. Boil for another minute and retest. Another method is the sheeting test: Dip a spoon into the boiling jam, and watch how it drips off the edge. If it falls in thick sheets instead of individual drops, you've hit the right consistency.

What if your jam doesn't set the way you hoped? Don't worry, it happens to everyone at some point. Sometimes it just needs time; pectin can take 24 to 48 hours to fully develop. But if it's still too runny after that, you can reprocess it by reheating and adding a little more pectin or acid to help it firm up.

Getting the perfect gel can take a little trial and error, but once you get the hang of it, you'll feel like a pro. Whether you like your jam thick and spreadable or a little on the looser side, understanding these simple tests will help you get the results you want every time.

# STEP-BY-STEP INSTRUCTIONS FOR WATER BATH CANNING

**Step 1:** *Gather and inspect equipment.*

Before you start canning, take a moment to gather everything you need. Having your tools laid out and ready will make the process smoother and more enjoyable. You'll need clean mason jars, new lids, and screw bands, along with a large, heavy-bottomed stockpot deep enough to fully submerge your jars. A canning rack is essential to keep jars elevated, allowing for even water circulation and preventing direct contact with the bottom of the pot, which could cause breakage. As you sort through your jars, check carefully for any chips or cracks. Damaged jars won't seal properly and could break during processing. Lids should always be brand-new to ensure a tight, reliable seal, while screw bands can be reused if they are rust-free and in good condition.

**Step 2:** *Wash and sterilize jars and lids.*

Cleanliness is key to safe canning. Wash your jars, lids, and bands in hot, soapy water, rinsing well to remove any soap residue. Even if they're brand-new, give them a thorough cleaning to eliminate dust or debris. To sterilize the jars, submerge them in simmering (not boiling) water for at least 10 minutes, keeping them hot until they're ready to be filled. This prevents thermal shock, which causes jars to crack when hot food is added to cold jars. While sterilizing jars, heat the lids in a separate pot of simmering (not boiling) water. This softens the sealing compound, helping the lids create a strong airtight bond once the jars cool.

**Step 3:** *Prepare canning pot.*

Fill your stockpot or water bath canner with enough water to cover the jars by at least 1 to 2 inches once they're submerged. Begin heating the water, bringing it to a simmer while you prepare your food. Starting with warm water helps speed up the process once the jars are filled and loaded into the canner.

**Step 4:** *Fill jars.*

Using a canning funnel to keep things neat, carefully ladle your prepared food into the hot jars, leaving ¼ inch to 1½ inches of headspace for jams and other high-acid foods, or as specified in your recipe. Headspace is crucial because it allows food to expand during processing and helps ensure a strong vacuum seal as the jars cool.

**Step 5:** *Remove air bubbles and adjust headspace.*

Before sealing, use a bubble remover tool (or a nonmetallic utensil like a chopstick) to gently stir the contents and release trapped air bubbles. Trapped air can affect the seal and cause spoilage over time. After removing bubbles, double-check the headspace and adjust, if necessary, by adding or removing food or liquid.

**Step 6:** *Wipe rims and secure lids.*

Once the jars are filled and the headspace is correct, wipe the rims with a clean, damp cloth or paper towel to remove any residue. Even a small amount of food or liquid on the rim interferes with sealing. Place the warmed lids on the jars, then screw on the bands fingertip-tight—snug but not overly tight. Overtightening prevents air from escaping during processing, which is necessary for a strong vacuum seal.

**Step 7:** *Load canner.*

Using a jar lifter, carefully place the filled jars into the canning rack inside your stockpot or water bath canner. Lower the rack (or jars) into the hot but not boiling water, ensuring there's at least 1 inch of water covering the tops of the jars.

**Step 8:** *Bring water to a rolling boil and start timing.*

Cover the canner with the lid and turn the heat to high. Wait until the water reaches a full rolling boil; only then should you start the processing timer according to your recipe. Maintaining a consistent boil for the full time is essential to properly heat and seal the jars. If the water level drops below the jar tops during processing, add more boiling water to keep them fully submerged. Adjust the processing time for altitude if needed (see page 198).

**Step 9:** *Remove jars and let cool.*

When the processing time is up, turn off the heat and remove the canner lid carefully, tilting it away from you to avoid steam burns. Let the jars rest in the hot water for 5 minutes before removing them. This prevents siphoning (liquid loss). Using a jar lifter, transfer the jars to a towel-lined surface, keeping them upright and undisturbed.

Once your jars are removed from the canner, it's important to let them cool upright and undisturbed for at least 12 to 24 hours. While it might be tempting to tilt them to check for a seal or drain excess water from the lid, doing so interferes with the vacuum-sealing process.

As a jar cools, the air inside contracts, pulling the lid down and creating a strong airtight seal. If a jar is placed on its side or turned upside down, liquid inside can seep between the lid and the rim, preventing a proper seal or introducing bacteria that causes spoilage. Keeping jars upright also ensures that any trapped air bubbles rise naturally to the top without affecting the consistency or safety of your preserves.

**Step 10:** *Check seals.*

After the jars have cooled completely, check the seals by pressing on the center of each lid. A properly sealed lid will be concave and not flex when pressed. If a lid pops up and down, the jar did not seal, and it should be refrigerated and used within 7 to 10 days.

**Step 11:** *Label and store.*

Label each jar with the date and contents before storing. Proper storage is just as important as proper processing. Keep jars in a cool, dark, dry place to maintain quality and safety (see page 19 for more on this). When stored correctly, some home-canned goods last for up to a year.

By following these guidelines, water bath canning is a reliable, safe way to enjoy seasonal produce year-round!

# TROUBLESHOOTING WATER BATH CANNING

Even the most seasoned canners run into occasional hiccups, so if something doesn't go quite right, don't be discouraged! Every batch is a learning experience, and most common canning issues have simple fixes. Let's go over a few things that might happen and how to prevent them next time.

## SIPHONING (LIQUID LOSS)

Ever opened your canner to find the liquid levels in your jars mysteriously lower than when you started? That's siphoning—when liquid is forced out of the jar during processing, sometimes leaving food exposed. You might also notice residue on the rim or under the lid.

**Why it happens:** Siphoning usually occurs because of sudden temperature changes or incorrect headspace. If jars are moved too quickly from hot water to a cooler environment, the rapid pressure shift can pull liquid out. Overfilling jars can also cause liquid to be pushed out during processing.

**How to fix it:** Let jars rest in the hot water for 5 minutes after processing before removing them. This allows them to adjust gradually to the temperature change. Also, make sure you maintain a steady boil the entire time and leave the amount of headspace specified in your recipe. This gives food room to expand without forcing liquid out.

## UNSEALED JARS

A properly sealed jar has a concave lid that doesn't flex when pressed. If the lid pops up and down when you touch it, the vacuum seal didn't take, meaning air may have gotten inside—and we don't want that!

**Why it happens:** The most common culprits are food residue on the jar rim, improper headspace, or overtightened bands. A bent lid or an uneven jar rim also prevents sealing.

**How to fix it:** Before placing the lids, wipe the rims with a clean, damp cloth to remove any residue—syrups, brine, or food particles can break the seal. Follow headspace guidelines exactly—too little space can cause food to seep under the lid, while too much can prevent proper suction. Screw on the bands fingertip-tight—just snug, not cranked down. If a jar doesn't seal within 24 hours, refrigerate it and use it within a week for items that spoil easily and up to a month or longer for jams, or reprocess it with a new lid.

## CLOUDY BRINE

If your pickling liquid looks cloudy instead of clear, don't worry; it's usually not spoilage, just a sign of minerals or additives in your ingredients.

**Why it happens:** The biggest culprits are anticaking agents in table salt and minerals in hard water. Table salt often contains additives to keep it from clumping in humid conditions, but those same additives can cause murkiness in your brine. Hard water, which is rich in calcium and magnesium, can also react with vinegar, leaving a cloudy residue.

**How to fix it:** Always use pickling salt or canning salt; these are pure salt without anticaking agents. If you have hard water, try using filtered or distilled water for your pickling liquid. If tap water is your only option, boil it first, then let it cool before using.

## FLOATING FOOD

Ever stored a jar of preserves and later found your pickles or peaches floating at the top, leaving the bottom half of the jar looking a little empty? That's floating food, and while it's not dangerous, it's not ideal for storage.

**Why it happens:** Floating happens when food isn't packed tightly enough, or when air bubbles trapped inside push it upward. Some fruits, like peaches and pears, are naturally buoyant, making them more prone to this issue.

**How to fix it:** Pack food firmly but not forcefully. You want enough room for liquid to circulate, but not so much space that food shifts during processing. Before sealing, use a bubble remover tool or a chopstick to stir the contents and release any hidden air pockets. This helps keep food evenly distributed.

There's nothing worse than hearing a jar crack in the canner. It's a heartbreaking sound but totally avoidable.

**Why it happens:** The most common reason for broken jars is thermal shock—when a cold jar is suddenly exposed to high heat. Hairline cracks or defects in the glass also cause jars to shatter during processing.

**How to fix it:** Always preheat jars before filling them, especially if you're adding hot liquids. Never place a cold jar into boiling water. Bring the water up to temperature gradually to prevent sudden temperature swings. Inspect jars carefully before using them, and discard any with small cracks or chips, even if they seem minor.

## PRACTICE RECIPE

# SIMPLE STRAWBERRY JAM
### EARLY SUMMER | WATER BATH | YIELD: 6 (8-OZ) HALF-PINT JARS

*Welcome to your first water bath canning project! This strawberry jam is perfect for beginners. The recipe is forgiving, and you'll practice key preservation techniques such as jar filling, bubble removal, and testing for proper sealing. Plus, capturing the taste of ripe summer strawberries to enjoy in the middle of winter is a gift we can give ourselves.*

### INGREDIENTS

5 cups fresh whole strawberries, hulled and mashed (see Tips)

1 package (1.75 oz) regular powdered fruit pectin

¼ cup bottled lemon juice

7 cups granulated sugar

### INSTRUCTIONS

1  Prepare jars for canning and keep warm. Wash and sterilize jars in boiling water for 10 minutes. Keep warm in oven. (See page 33.)

2  In a large, deep saucepan, combine mashed strawberries, pectin, and lemon juice. Bring to a full boil over high heat, stirring constantly to prevent sticking.

3  Carefully add all of the sugar. Stirring constantly, return the mixture to a rolling boil. Boil hard for 1 minute. Using a slotted spoon, skim off foam (see Tips). Turn off heat.

4  Ladle the hot jam into prepared jars, leaving ¼-inch headspace. Remove bubbles using a bubble remover (see page 34). Wipe rims clean with a damp cloth or paper towel.

5  Place lids on jars, then screw on bands and tighten just until fingertip-tight (see page 34).

6  Using a jar lifter, place jars in canner rack. Submerge rack in boiling water, ensuring jars are covered by at least 1 inch of hot water. Cover canner with lid and bring water to a rolling boil.

7  Process jars for 10 minutes (adjust for altitude, if needed; see page 198). At end of processing time, turn off heat and remove lid.

8  Once water has stopped boiling, use jar lifter to carefully remove jars, without tilting, and place on a towel.

9  Let jars cool, undisturbed, for 12 to 24 hours. Test the seals by gently pressing down on the center of the lids. They should not flex (see page 35).

## TIPS

Mashing the berries by hand with a potato masher makes quick work of breaking them down while leaving some delicious fruit texture in your jam.

Stirring a scant ½ teaspoon of olive oil or butter into the jam while cooking helps reduce foam, making skimming easier.

Always use bottled lemon juice for canning, as it has a consistent acidity level, ensuring your jam is safe for long-term storage. Fresh lemons vary in acidity, which affects preservation.

CHAPTER 4

PRESSURE
CANNING

In 2020, I received my first pressure canner. At the time, I had already built plenty of confidence with water bath canning, but pressure canning? That felt like stepping into a new world. I had all the same thoughts you probably have right now: *Isn't it dangerous? What if I do something wrong?* After a few successful batches, I realized pressure canning is just another skill—one that, once mastered, opens a new range of possibilities. Unlike water bath canning, which is limited to high-acid foods, pressure canning allows you to safely preserve low-acid foods like vegetables, meats, soups, and broths. And trust me, stocking your pantry with shelf-stable homemade broth or jars of garden-fresh green beans is an incredibly rewarding feeling.

So, what makes pressure canning different—and why do you need it? The answer comes down to acidity and temperature.

Low-acid foods—those with a pH above 4.6—don't have enough natural acidity to prevent bacterial growth, particularly *Clostridium botulinum*, the bacteria responsible for botulism. These foods include:

- Vegetables (green beans, carrots, potatoes)
- Meats, poultry, and seafood
- Soups, stews, broths, and stocks

While boiling water (used in water bath canning) kills many bacteria, it's not hot enough to destroy botulism spores, which require temperatures of 240°F to 250°F to be neutralized. The only way to achieve those temperatures at home is with pressurized steam, which is exactly what a pressure canner is designed to create.

## HOW PRESSURE CANNING WORKS

At its core, pressure canning is all about using steam under pressure to raise the temperature inside the canner beyond what boiling water alone achieves. Here's how it works:

1. The sealed canner traps steam. Once filled and sealed jars are placed inside and the canner lid is locked, the canner, which contains water, is heated, creating steam.

2. Pressure builds, increasing the internal temperature. When the vent is closed, pressure increases, raising the boiling point of water beyond 212°F.

3. Heat penetrates the jars, killing bacteria. The combination of high heat and sustained pressure ensures the food inside the jars reaches a safe temperature.

4. A vacuum seal forms as jars cool. Once processing is complete, the canner is allowed to cool naturally. As the jars cool, a vacuum forms, sealing them for safe, long-term storage.

## MYTHS VS. FACTS: PRESSURE CANNING

Pressure canning is a powerful tool for preserving low-acid foods, but myths and misconceptions often make it seem intimidating. Let's separate fact from fiction and put your fears to rest.

**MYTH:** Pressure canners are dangerous and can explode.

**FACT:** Modern pressure canners are equipped with multiple safety mechanisms, such as vent locks, overpressure plugs, and weighted or dial gauges. Following the manufacturer's instructions and regular maintenance ensure safe operation.

**MYTH:** Pressure canning is too complicated for beginners.

**FACT:** While pressure canning requires attention to detail, the process is straightforward once you understand the basics. Trusted recipes and step-by-step instructions make it easy to learn.

**MYTH:** All pressure canners require constant monitoring.

**FACT:** Weighted-gauge pressure canners maintain pressure automatically and need less supervision compared to dial-gauge models. Choose a canner that fits your comfort level.

**MYTH:** Canned food lasts forever.

**FACT:** Pressure-canned food can last for 2 to 5 years when stored properly; regular rotation and inspection ensure quality and safety.

Understanding the facts about pressure canning helps alleviate fears and empowers you to confidently preserve nutritious and delicious meals for your pantry.

## BUILT-IN SAFETY FEATURES

Modern pressure canners are designed with multiple safety mechanisms, including:

- Locking lids that prevent opening under pressure
- Overpressure plugs that release excess steam, if needed
- Vent pipes that regulate steam flow for stable pressure

As long as you follow the manufacturer's instructions for use, you can be confident that your pressure canner will operate safely and effectively.

## WHAT NOT TO PRESSURE CAN

While pressure canning works for most low-acid foods, some things just don't turn out well.

**Summer squash and puréed pumpkin:** These vegetables become too soft and dense, preventing proper heat penetration during canning. Instead, freeze or pickle them.

**Dairy, pasta, and rice:** These ingredients don't can well because they interfere with heat distribution during canning and break down over time.

**Thickened soups and stews:** Thickened soups and stews also interfere with proper heat penetration during canning. Always can broths and thin soups. You can thicken them later when reheating.

## THE PROBLEM WITH PURÉED PUMPKIN

Pumpkin is a thick, starchy vegetable, and when blended into a purée, it becomes even denser. That might not seem like a big deal, but it's a problem when it comes to pressure canning. The process relies on steam heat reaching every part of the jar evenly to kill bacteria like *Clostridium botulinum*. If the food inside is too thick, heat can't fully penetrate the center, creating cold spots where bacteria survive.

The USDA has tested home canning methods for pumpkin purée and found no way to guarantee safe, even heat distribution. That's why you won't find any approved pressure-canning recipes for pumpkin purée—it's just too risky. Instead, the best way to preserve pumpkin is to can it in cubes (which allows heat to circulate properly) or freeze purée for later use.

## WHAT ABOUT SUMMER SQUASH?

Summer squash—including zucchini, yellow squash, and pattypan—comes with a different problem: too much water. These squash varieties have a high moisture content and delicate texture, which means that after pressure canning, they tend to break down into an unappetizing mush. But the bigger issue is that when overcooked, squash becomes too thick inside the jar, much like puréed pumpkin. This prevents proper heat circulation and makes it unsafe for pressure canning. Because of these concerns, the USDA does not recommend canning summer squash—no matter how tempting that mountain of zucchini might be.

## SAFE ALTERNATIVES FOR PRESERVING PUMPKIN AND SQUASH

Just because you can't pressure can puréed pumpkin or summer squash doesn't mean you're out of options. Here are a few safer (and better!) ways to preserve them:

**FREEZING:** The best way to store puréed pumpkin and summer squash is to freeze them. Portion into containers or use ice-cube trays for easy, grab-and-go servings. This keeps the texture intact and ensures safety.

**PICKLING:** If you're set on canning summer squash, go for zucchini pickles or squash relish using a tested water bath canning recipe. The added acidity makes them safe for long-term storage.

**CANNING PUMPKIN CUBES:** While puréed pumpkin isn't safe for canning, pumpkin cubes are! Cut them into uniform pieces, pressure can them in water following a tested recipe, and mash or purée them when you're ready to use them.

## WHAT ABOUT MEAT?

Pressure-canning meat is a great way to utilize every part of an animal without waste, and you'll find tested recipes for assorted types of protein in this book. However, because meat requires specific handling and strict adherence to safety guidelines, there are a few important things to know before you get started.

First, always trim excess fat before canning. Fat doesn't process the same way as lean meat. It interferes with heat penetration, prevents proper sealing, and even leads to spoilage over time. For the best results, choose lean cuts and remove as much fat as possible.

Second, skip the thickeners. It might be tempting to can meat in a gravy or sauce, but thickeners like flour, cornstarch, and even dairy-based ingredients slow down heat transfer, making it difficult to ensure the food is evenly processed. Instead, can meat in broth, water, or its own juices, then thicken the liquid after opening the jar when you're ready to cook.

Lastly, you have a choice between hot-pack and raw-pack methods. With hot packing, meat is lightly cooked before being packed into jars, which helps remove air pockets and results in better texture. Raw packing, on the other hand, involves placing raw meat directly into jars without precooking. While both methods are USDA approved, hot packing tends to yield more flavor and better-textured results.

Pressure-canning meat is a fantastic way to stock your pantry with ready-to-use proteins, whether for quick weeknight meals or long-term food storage. As with all pressure canning, follow tested recipes carefully to ensure safe and delicious results!

## FUNDAMENTALS FOR SAFE PRESSURE CANNING

If you're new to pressure canning, all the talk about "venting steam" and "monitoring PSI" may sound daunting (you'll learn more about this in the coming pages), but I promise, once you understand the process, it's completely manageable. Pressure canning is all about controlling heat and pressure to ensure your food is safe for long-term storage. Following a few key safety steps will set you up for success and help you feel confident about using your canner.

### GAUGE TESTING: WHY ACCURACY MATTERS

If you're using a dial-gauge pressure canner (like a Presto model), you need to check the gauge once a year to make sure it's reading pressure correctly. An inaccurate gauge could mean your food isn't reaching the temperature needed to destroy harmful bacteria. Most county extension offices will test gauges for free, or check with the manufacturer for calibration services.

If you have a weighted-gauge canner (like an All American model), good news—these don't require testing because they regulate pressure with a weight instead of a dial.

### PROPER VENTING: THE 10-MINUTE RULE

Before sealing the canner, you must allow steam to vent for 10 minutes. This step removes trapped air, ensuring the inside of the canner is filled with pure steam, which distributes heat evenly. If air is left inside, the canner may not reach the correct temperature, putting your food at risk. Think of it like preheating your oven. You wouldn't put a cake into a cold oven and expect it to bake correctly, right?

To vent your canner, simply leave the vent open (or remove the weight, depending on your model) when you start heating it. Once you see a steady stream of steam coming from the vent, set a timer for 10 minutes before sealing the canner.

## USE TESTED RECIPES: NO GUESSWORK ALLOWED

Pressure canning isn't the time to experiment. Unlike cooking, where you adjust ingredients to taste, canning safety relies on scientifically tested recipes that ensure food is heated all the way through. Always follow guidelines from trusted sources such as the USDA, Ball, or university extension offices. Changing ingredients—especially in low-acid foods—affects heat penetration and safety.

## MONITORING PRESSURE: KEEP THINGS STEADY

Once your canner is sealed and pressurized, you'll need to maintain steady pressure throughout the entire processing time. If the pressure drops below the recommended level (measured in pounds per square inch, or PSI), the food may not have been processed safely. If this happens, you must restart the timer from the beginning—yes, even if you were 30 minutes into the process! If the pressure rises too high, excess steam will be released through the regulator. Avoid wild fluctuations—a consistent heat setting will help keep the temperature steady.

Since air pressure changes at higher elevations, you'll need to adjust your PSI if you live above 1,000 feet (see page 199). (Your recipe will tell you how much to adjust for your altitude.)

## COOLING NATURALLY: NO SHORTCUTS

Once processing is complete, the canner must cool naturally before you open it. This means no force-cooling it with cold water or removing the weight too soon, and no lifting the lid until the pressure is completely back to zero.

Forcing a canner to cool too quickly causes liquid to siphon out of jars, weakens seals, or even causes the jars to break due to sudden temperature changes. Instead, turn off the heat and let the canner sit undisturbed. It may take 30 to 60 minutes for the pressure to drop fully—be patient!

## CHOOSING THE RIGHT WEIGHT FOR YOUR PRESSURE CANNER

If you have a dial-gauge pressure canner, you don't need to change weights—just adjust the heat to maintain the correct PSI. Dial gauges must be tested annually for accuracy, while weighted gauges don't require calibration. If you're using a weighted-gauge pressure canner, the weight you place on the air vent (also called the vent pipe) controls the amount of pressure inside the canner. Different recipes call for specific pressures, and your altitude affects what weight you should use.

### HOW IT WORKS

The weight acts like a pressure regulator. When the canner reaches the correct pressure, the weight will rock or jiggle to release excess steam, maintaining a steady internal temperature. If you use the incorrect weight, your food may not process safely.

### WHAT WEIGHT SHOULD YOU USE?

Most weighted-gauge canners come with a three-piece regulator that allows you to select 5, 10, or 15 PSI. Here's how to determine which one you need:

For altitudes of 0 to 1,000 feet → Use 10 PSI (most common setting)

For altitudes above 1,000 feet → Use 15 PSI (higher elevation requires more pressure to reach safe temperatures)

If you're unsure of your altitude, look it up online or check a topographic map. Your canning manual will also include a chart to help you make adjustments.

Understanding the correct weight to use ensures your food is processed at safe temperatures, which means a pantry full of reliably preserved, shelf-stable food!

## MAINTAINING AND CLEANING YOUR PRESSURE CANNER

A well-maintained pressure canner is the heart of safe, successful home canning. Keeping it clean and in good working order ensures that it performs reliably, maintains accurate pressure, and lasts for years—maybe even generations. Taking a few simple steps after each use will keep your canner running smoothly so you can focus on what really matters: filling your pantry with homemade, shelf-stable goodness.

### ROUTINE CLEANING AFTER EACH USE

A little care after each canning session goes a long way in preventing mineral buildup, food residue, and corrosion. Think of it as wiping down your stovetop after cooking—just a small habit that keeps the canning process running smoothly.

1. Wash the canner body and lid. Never submerge your canner lid in water. This damages internal components. Use warm, soapy water and a soft cloth or sponge to clean both the inside and outside. Skip abrasive scrubbers or harsh cleaners, as they can scratch the surface.

2. Clean the vent pipe and safety valve. These tiny openings regulate pressure by releasing steam. Run a pipe cleaner or a small brush through them to clear any debris. A blocked vent pipe could cause pressure issues, so don't skip this step!

3. Check the sealing ring (if your canner has one). Some models use a rubber or silicone gasket to create an airtight seal. Over time, this can dry out, crack, or stretch. If it feels brittle, replace it before your next canning session.

4. Dry the canner thoroughly. Leftover moisture leads to rust, especially in aluminum canners. After washing, dry everything completely before storing.

### DEEP CLEANING AND REMOVING MINERAL BUILDUP

If you have hard water, you may notice a white or cloudy residue forming inside your canner over time. This is caused by mineral deposits, and, while harmless, it's best to remove them before they build up too much.

1. Fill the canner with a 50/50 mix of water and white vinegar, then bring it to a low boil for 10 to 15 minutes.

2. Let it cool, then wipe away any loosened residue with a soft cloth.

3. If you have an aluminum canner, avoid harsh chemicals; they can damage the metal. Stick to vinegar and gentle scrubbing.

## CALIBRATING AND TESTING YOUR PRESSURE CANNER

Just like a kitchen thermometer, a pressure canner must be accurate to do its job properly. If the pressure inside your canner isn't correct, your food may not reach the necessary temperature for safe preservation.

**Dial-gauge canners (like Presto models):** These use a dial to measure pressure, and the gauge must be tested annually. Over time, gauges can drift, leading to under- or overprocessing. Many county extension offices offer free gauge testing, or check with the manufacturer for calibration services.

**Weighted-gauge canners (like All American models):** These do not require testing since the weight itself regulates pressure. However, it's still important to inspect the parts regularly and replace any worn components.

## STORAGE TIPS TO KEEP YOUR CANNER IN TOP SHAPE

A well-cared-for pressure canner will last a lifetime (or longer!). When canning season wraps up, store your canner properly to keep it ready for next time.

1. Store with the lid off. Never lock the lid onto the canner when storing it. This traps moisture inside, leading to rust and odors.

2. Keep the sealing ring loose. If your canner has a rubber gasket, remove it and store it separately to prevent warping.

3. Choose a dry storage spot. Avoid damp areas, as excess humidity causes corrosion over time.

A pressure canner is one of the best investments you can make in your kitchen. It allows you to safely preserve food for years of home-cooked convenience. A little routine maintenance goes a long way. As I tell my son, "Take care of your canning tools, and they'll take care of you."

# STEP-BY-STEP INSTRUCTIONS FOR PRESSURE CANNING

Whether you're preserving vegetables, stews, or broths, pressure canning is the safest way to store low-acid foods for long-term shelf stability. Pressure canning sounds overwhelming, but by breaking down the process into simple steps, it becomes straightforward and rewarding. Take your time, follow tested recipes, and don't be afraid to get comfortable with your pressure canner.

**Step 1:** *Gather your equipment.*

A well-prepared workspace makes canning smoother and safer. Before you begin, make sure you have everything you need. A pressure canner with a canning rack is essential. The rack prevents jars from sitting directly on the bottom of the canner, allowing heat to circulate properly. You'll also need mason jars, lids, and bands. Always use new lids to ensure a good seal, but bands can be reused if they are rust-free and undamaged. A jar lifter, canning funnel, ladle, and bubble remover make handling hot jars and filling them much easier. Lastly, keep a timer handy, as accurate processing times are critical for food safety (for a detailed list of essential tools, see page 13).

**Step 2:** *Inspect and prepare equipment.*

A quick equipment check before canning prevents issues later. If using a dial-gauge canner, check that the gauge has been tested for accuracy within the past year (see page 44). Inspect the canner for cracks, worn seals, or loose parts, and ensure all components are in working order. Wash jars, lids, and bands in hot, soapy water, even if they are brand-new. This removes any dust or factory residue. Keep jars warm until ready to fill. This prevents thermal shock when hot food is added. You can do this by keeping them in hot water, a warm oven, or a dishwasher's heated dry setting.

**Step 3:** *Prepare ingredients and fill jars.*

Follow a tested recipe exactly. Pressure canning is not the time for improvisation. Adjusting ingredients or processing times results in unsafe food.

Prepare ingredients as directed in your recipe. Some foods require peeling, chopping, or blanching, while others may be packed raw. When filling jars, leave 1 to 1½ inches of headspace (the empty space between the food and the lid) to allow for expansion during processing.

Remove trapped air bubbles by running a bubble remover (or a nonmetallic utensil like a chopstick) around the inside of the jar. Wipe rims with a damp cloth to remove any food particles that could prevent a proper seal. Place lids on jars and tighten bands fingertip-tight—snug but not overly tight—so air escapes during processing.

**Step 4:** *Add water and load jars.*

Unlike water bath canning, pressure canning does not fully submerge jars. It uses steam and pressurized heat instead. Pour 2 to 3 inches of water into the canner. (Check your model's manual for exact recommendations.) Then arrange sealed jars upright on the canner rack, making sure they do not touch one another or the sides of the canner. Steam must circulate freely around the jars to ensure even heating. If jars are too close together, heat distribution may be uneven, and food may not reach a safe processing temperature. Additionally, jars can bump into one another during processing, increasing the risk of breakage. If double-stacking jars, place a second canning rack between layers to allow steam to flow properly.

**Step 5:** *Heat canner and vent steam (critical!).*

Venting your pressure canner is one of the most important safety steps in the process. It ensures that all air is expelled, leaving only steam inside, which is necessary to create the correct pressurized environment.

After locking the lid securely, turn the heat on your stove to high. Watch for a steady stream of steam escaping from the vent pipe. This means the air inside is being pushed out. Once you see continuous steam, set a timer for 10 minutes, and allow the canner to vent fully. This step is crucial because any trapped air causes uneven heating, leading to unsafe food.

If the vent pipe is sealed too soon, air pockets remain inside, creating false pressure readings. Your gauge might read 11 PSI, but if air is mixed in with the steam, the actual temperature inside the canner may be too low to safely kill bacteria. That's why it's essential to complete this step every time. Proper venting ensures accurate pressure, even heating, and food safety. Simply put, always wait until the pressure gauge reads zero before removing the lid or regulator, and tilt the lid away from your face when opening the canner.

**Step 6:** *Add the regulator and monitor pressure.*

Once the canner has vented for 10 minutes, place the pressure regulator (weight) onto the vent pipe. This allows pressure to build inside the canner. Wait until the canner reaches the correct pressure for your altitude.

| ALTITUDE (FEET) | DIAL GAUGE (PSI) | WEIGHTED GAUGE (PSI) |
|:---:|:---:|:---:|
| 0 to 1,000 | 11 | 10 |
| 1,001 to 2,000 | 12 | 11 |
| 2,001 to 4,000 | 13 | 12 |
| 4,001 to 6,000 | 14 | 13 |
| 6,001 to 8,000 | 15 | 14 |

Begin timing only when the correct pressure is reached. Maintain steady heat, as pressure fluctuations affect safety. If the pressure drops below the required PSI, you must restart the processing time from the beginning (see page 45).

**Step 7:** *Maintain steady pressure.*

Once your canner has reached the correct pressure, your job isn't over yet. You need to maintain steady heat to keep the pressure consistent throughout the entire processing time. Fluctuations in pressure affect both safety and food quality, so small adjustments may be necessary as your canner runs. As soon as your gauge or weighted regulator shows the correct pressure for your altitude, reduce the heat slightly—just enough to keep the pressure steady without dropping below the required level. Every stove is different, so this step may take some trial and error. If the pressure starts creeping too high, lower the heat gradually rather than making sudden adjustments. If the pressure drops below the required PSI, you must restart the processing time from the beginning to ensure food safety.

If your canner is running under pressure, food may not reach the required temperature for safe preservation, increasing the risk of spoilage or botulism. Running it over pressure doesn't add extra safety. In fact, it causes food quality issues, including excessive siphoning (liquid loss) or jar seal failure. Rapid pressure changes force liquid out of jars, leaving food partially exposed, which may shorten shelf life.

If you're using a weighted-gauge canner, the regulator should move in a controlled rhythm. Different brands have slightly different "jiggle" patterns; consult your manual. If the weight is rocking too forcefully or steam is escaping constantly, reduce the heat slightly. A gentle, rhythmic movement means you're maintaining the correct pressure.

Remember: If the pressure drops below the required level at any time, you must bring it back up and restart the full processing time. Pressure canning relies on one continuous, uninterrupted cycle at the correct pressure to ensure food safety.

**Step 8:** *Turn off heat and let the canner cool naturally.*

Once the processing time is complete, turn off the heat and let the canner sit undisturbed until the pressure gauge reads zero (this may take 30 to 60 minutes). Never force-cool the canner by running cold water over it. This causes liquid loss or jar breakage. When opening the lid, tilt it away from your face to avoid steam burns.

**Step 9:** *Remove jars and test seals.*

Using a jar lifter, carefully transfer the jars to a towel-lined surface. Keep them upright and do not tilt or turn them upside down, even if there's water on the lid. Let them cool, undisturbed, for 12 to 24 hours. Moving them too soon can break the seal. After cooling, test the seals by pressing the center of each lid. If it doesn't flex, the jar is sealed properly. If it pops up and down, refrigerate and use the contents within a few days.

**Step 10:** *Label and store jars.*

Once jars are sealed, label them with the contents and date. Store in a cool, dark, dry place to ensure freshness. Avoid direct sunlight or humidity, as this affects shelf life.

## TROUBLESHOOTING PRESSURE CANNING

There are a few key differences between pressure canning and water bath canning, and understanding common issues will help you feel more confident every time you preserve food. Here's how to troubleshoot some of the most frequent problems.

**Pressure dropped during processing?** Restart the processing time from the beginning once the pressure is restored.

**Jars didn't seal?** Check for food residue on rims or damaged lids. Reprocess within 24 hours or refrigerate and use within a few days.

**Too much liquid loss?** This is siphoning, often caused by rapid cooling or pressure fluctuations. Next time, let the canner cool naturally.

**Pressure canning with hard water?** If you have hard water, you may notice a white, chalky film forming on the outside of your jars after pressure canning. This residue is caused by mineral deposits (primarily calcium and magnesium) that remain behind as the water evaporates. While this doesn't affect the safety of your canned food, it leaves jars looking cloudy or streaked. To minimize hard water deposits when pressure canning, try one of these methods:

1. Add white vinegar to the canner water. Many canners recommend adding 1 to 2 tablespoons of white vinegar to the water inside the pressure canner before processing. The vinegar helps dissolve minerals and reduces buildup on jars.

## PRESSURE CANNING WITH CONFIDENCE

Pressure canning may seem intimidating, but understanding what's normal will build your confidence and ensure safe preservation.

### NORMAL SOUNDS AND SIGHTS

**HISSING AND STEAM:** A gentle hissing sound and visible steam during venting are normal.

**REGULATOR MOVEMENT:** Weighted gauges may rock or jiggle rhythmically (check the manufacturer's instructions).

**QUIET PROCESSING:** Once pressure stabilizes, the canner will maintain a steady, quiet operation.

**CONSISTENT VENTING:** A steady steam column should vent for 10 minutes before you apply the regulator.

### GAUGE BEHAVIOR

**DIAL GAUGES:** Should rise steadily. A wobbly needle may indicate a faulty gauge (test annually; see page 44).

**WEIGHTED GAUGES:** Should rock/jiggle steadily. If movement stops or is too frequent, adjust the heat (see page 46).

### WARNING SIGNS

**SUDDEN PRESSURE LOSS:** If the PSI drops, restart the timing once the pressure is restored.

**EXCESSIVE STEAM RELEASE:** Continuous venting through the safety valve may signal overpressure—turn off the heat and let the canner cool (see page 52).

**SIDE STEAM LEAKS:** Misaligned lids or damaged seals may cause escaping steam. Check the sealing ring (see page 47).

*Continued on following page …*

2. Wipe the jars after processing. If residue remains after canning, wipe the jars with a vinegar-dampened cloth to remove any lingering film.

3. Use filtered or softened water. If possible, fill your canner with filtered, distilled, or preboiled softened water to reduce mineral buildup (for more details, see page 47).

page 47

**TROUBLESHOOTING**

**OVERPRESSURE:** If the safety plug releases steam, turn off the heat and let it cool before handling.

**CANNER LID STUCK:** Ensure all pressure is released before attempting to open it.

With these insights, you'll gain confidence in pressure canning—making preservation safe, predictable, and stress-free!

**PRACTICE RECIPE**

# CANNED GREEN BEANS
**SUMMER | PRESSURE CANNING | YIELD: 4 (16-OZ) PINT JARS**

*Perfect for soups, casseroles, or simple side dishes, this beginner-friendly recipe will help you build confidence with pressure canning. You'll practice proper hot packing, venting, and sealing techniques while ensuring safe, long-term storage of fresh green beans. (Note: I include instructions for raw packing the beans in the Variation on page 55, if you want to give that a try too.)*

**INGREDIENTS**

2 pounds fresh green beans

1 tsp canning salt per jar (optional)

Boiling water, to pour over beans

**INSTRUCTIONS**

1 Prepare jars, bands, and lids for canning and keep warm (see page 49).

2 Prepare beans for canning: Wash, trim, and de-string the beans. Cut into 1-inch pieces. Bring a large pot of water to a boil. Add prepared beans and boil for 2 minutes. (This is called "blanching.") Drain.

3 Pack the blanched beans tightly in prepared jars, leaving 1-inch headspace. Add 1 tsp canning salt per jar (if using).

4 Pour boiling water over the beans, maintaining 1-inch headspace.

5   Remove air bubbles, wipe rims, and secure lids fingertip-tight (see page 49).

6   Fill the pressure canner with 2 to 3 inches of water. (Check your model's manual for exact recommendations.)

7   Load jars into the pressure canner, ensuring they don't touch. Secure the canner lid and turn heat to high.

8   Once the canner is steaming, allow it to vent steam for 10 minutes before installing the pressure regulator (see page 50).

9   Bring the canner to the correct PSI for your altitude (see page 199). Process jars for 20 minutes. (Start timer only when the canner reaches the correct pressure.)

10  Allow canner to cool naturally before opening (see page 52).

11  Let jars cool, undisturbed, for 12 to 24 hours. Check seals on cooled jars. Lids should not flex.

---

TIP

Precooking the beans slightly helps them retain their texture during processing. Also, avoid overpacking jars. Green beans need a bit of space to allow even heat penetration.

---

VARIATION

**To raw pack beans:** Skip blanching the beans in Step 2. Pack raw beans directly into jars, leaving 1-inch headspace. Add boiling water to cover, maintaining 1-inch headspace. Then proceed with Step 5. Note that while raw packing beans may be quicker, it does yield a softer texture.

# PART 2

# ESSENTIAL RECIPES

Chapter 5: Fruit                               58

Chapter 6: Vegetables                          78

Chapter 7: Sauces and Chutneys                 114

Chapter 8: Broths, Stocks, and Soups           138

Chapter 9: One-Jar Meals                       168

Chapter 10: Desserts in Jars                   188

CHAPTER 5

# FRUIT

| | | | | |
|---|---|---|---|---|
| Blueberry Jam | 60 | Apple Butter | 68 |
| Peach Preserves | 61 | Orange Marmalade | 70 |
| Pear Preserves | 62 | Low-Sugar Berry Preserves | 72 |
| Blackberry Preserves | 63 | Nectarine Jam | 73 |
| Cherry Preserves | 64 | Honey-Sweetened Berry Jam | 74 |
| Plum Jam | 65 | Pineapple Jalapeño Jelly | 75 |
| Raspberry Jam | 66 | Fig and Orange Conserve | 76 |
| Grape Jelly | 67 | Mango Lime Butter | 77 |

# TESTING FOR THE PERFECT CONSISTENCY

Achieving the right consistency when preserving jams, jellies, and marmalades requires precision and patience. The following three methods will help you determine when you've reached the perfect setting point while cooking.

## THE SPOON TEST (FOR JELLIES AND MARMALADES ONLY)

This test helps determine if your jelly or marmalade has the right texture before you move on to jarring.

1. Use a spoon to lift a small amount of the cooked preserves above the pot.
2. Let the preserve slide back into the pot.
3. If it drips in a wide sheet instead of separate drops, it's likely ready. If it's still too thin and drips in separate drops, cook for 2 to 5 additional minutes, then test again.
4. For accuracy, always confirm with the cold plate test before jarring.

## THE TEMPERATURE TEST

Using a candy thermometer is a precise way to check if your preserves are ready.

1. Clip the thermometer to the side of your pot, ensuring it doesn't touch the bottom.
2. Cook the jam or jelly until it reaches 220°F (or 8°F above your local boiling point).
3. Once the mixture reaches this temperature, maintain it for at least 1 minute before testing with the cold plate method.

## THE COLD PLATE TEST

1. Before starting your recipe, place a small plate in the freezer so it's ready when you need it.
2. Once your jam or jelly has cooked for the recommended time, drop a small spoonful onto the chilled plate.
3. Let it sit undisturbed for 30 seconds, then run your finger through the center.
4. If it wrinkles and holds the line, it's ready for jarring.
5. If it runs back together smoothly, continue cooking for 2 to 3 additional minutes, then test again.

By using temperature as a guide, the spoon test for an early warning, and the cold plate test for final confirmation, you'll achieve the perfect consistency every time!

> ### QUICK TIP FOR REDUCING FOAM
>
> When making jams and preserves, adding a small amount of butter or oil helps reduce foam formation. Simply stir in ½ tsp of unsalted butter or a few drops of neutral oil at the start of cooking. This helps break the surface tension, minimizing foam. However, if foam still forms, skim it off with a slotted spoon for a clearer jam.

# BLUEBERRY JAM

**SUMMER | WATER BATH | YIELD: 8 (8-OZ) HALF-PINT JARS**

*Thanks to the natural pectin in blueberries, blueberry jam sets beautifully, making this an ideal recipe for beginners. For the best flavor, use plump, peak-season berries.*

## INGREDIENTS

6 cups fresh blueberries
(approx. 3 pounds), crushed

4 tbsp bottled lemon juice

2 tbsp powdered pectin

5 cups granulated sugar

## INSTRUCTIONS

1   Fill your water canner roughly three-quarters full of water. Bring to a boil over high heat.

2   Prepare jars, bands, and lids for canning and keep warm (see page 33).

3   In a large, deep saucepan, combine crushed blueberries, lemon juice, and pectin. Bring to a full boil over high heat, stirring constantly to prevent sticking.

4   Carefully add all of the sugar. Stirring constantly, return the mixture to a rolling boil. Boil hard for 1 minute. Test for doneness using the cold plate or spoon test (see page 59). Using a slotted spoon, skim off any foam that forms on the surface. Turn off heat.

5   Ladle the hot jam into prepared jars, leaving ¼-inch headspace. Remove bubbles using a bubble remover (see page 34).

6   Using a clean, damp cloth or paper towel, wipe rims clean. Place sterilized lids on jars. Then screw on bands and tighten just until fingertip-tight (see page 34).

7   Using a jar lifter, place jars in canner rack. Submerge rack in boiling water, ensuring jars are covered by at least 1 inch of water (see page 34). Cover canner with lid and bring water to a rolling boil.

8   Process jars for 10 minutes (adjust for altitude, if needed; see page 198). At end of processing time, turn off heat and remove lid.

9   Once water has stopped boiling, use jar lifter to carefully remove jars, without tilting, and place on a towel.

10  Let jars cool, undisturbed, for 12 to 24 hours. Once completely cool, test the seals by gently pressing down on the center of the lids—they should not flex (see page 35).

# PEACH PRESERVES

SUMMER | WATER BATH | YIELD: 7 (8-OZ) HALF-PINT JARS

*Every summer my grandmother Alberta's kitchen filled with the scent of simmering peaches and warm sugar. To her, a well-stocked pantry was a sign of love, and no preserve was more cherished than these golden jars. Serve over warm biscuits, swirl into oatmeal, or enjoy straight from the jar.*

## INGREDIENTS

6 cups peeled, pitted, and chopped peaches (approx. 4 pounds)

¼ cup bottled lemon juice

3 tbsp powdered pectin

5 cups granulated sugar

## INSTRUCTIONS

1   Fill your water canner roughly three-quarters full of water. Bring to a boil over high heat.

2   Prepare jars, bands, and lids for canning and keep warm (see page 33).

3   In a large, deep saucepan, combine prepared peaches, lemon juice, and pectin. Bring to a full boil over high heat, stirring constantly to prevent sticking.

4   Carefully add all of the sugar. Stirring constantly, return the mixture to a rolling boil. Boil hard for 1 minute. Test for doneness using the cold plate or spoon test (see page 59). Using a slotted spoon, skim off any foam that forms on the surface. Turn off heat.

5   Ladle the hot preserves into prepared jars, leaving ¼-inch headspace. Remove bubbles using a bubble remover (see page 34).

6   Using a clean, damp cloth or paper towel, wipe rims clean. Place sterilized lids on jars. Then screw on bands and tighten just until fingertip-tight (see page 34).

7   Using a jar lifter, place jars in canner rack. Submerge rack in boiling water, ensuring jars are covered by at least 1 inch of water (see page 34). Cover canner with lid and bring water to a rolling boil.

8   Process jars for 10 minutes (adjust for altitude, if needed; see page 198). At end of processing time, turn off heat and remove lid.

9   Once water has stopped boiling, use jar lifter to carefully remove jars, without tilting, and place on a towel.

10  Let jars cool, undisturbed, for 12 to 24 hours. Once completely cool, test the seals by gently pressing down on the center of the lids—they should not flex (see page 35).

# PEAR PRESERVES

FALL | WATER BATH | YIELD: 7 (8-OZ) HALF-PINT JARS

*There's something deeply comforting about preserved pears—their soft, syrupy sweetness captures the essence of fall. These pears are best enjoyed spooned over warm toast or drizzled as a glaze over roasted meats. For a touch of warmth, stir in a pinch of nutmeg, cinnamon, or cardamom.*

## INGREDIENTS

6 cups peeled, cored, and chopped pears (4 pounds)

4 tbsp bottled lemon juice

3 tbsp powdered pectin

5 cups granulated sugar

## INSTRUCTIONS

1  Fill your water canner roughly three-quarters full of water. Bring to a boil over high heat.

2  Prepare jars, bands, and lids for canning and keep warm (see page 33).

3  In a large, deep saucepan, combine chopped pears, lemon juice, and pectin. Bring to a full boil over high heat, stirring constantly to prevent sticking.

4  Carefully add all of the sugar. Stirring constantly, return the mixture to a rolling boil. Boil hard for 1 minute. Test for doneness using the cold plate or spoon test (see page 59). Using a slotted spoon, skim off any foam that forms on the surface. Turn off heat.

5  Ladle the hot preserves into prepared jars, leaving ¼-inch headspace. Remove bubbles using a bubble remover (see page 34).

6  Using a clean, damp cloth or paper towel, wipe rims clean. Place sterilized lids on jars. Then screw on bands and tighten just until fingertip-tight (see page 34).

7  Using a jar lifter, place jars in canner rack. Submerge rack in boiling water, ensuring jars are covered by at least 1 inch of water (see page 34). Cover canner with lid and bring water to a rolling boil.

8  Process jars for 15 minutes (adjust for altitude, if needed; see page 198). At end of processing time, turn off heat and remove lid.

9  Once water has stopped boiling, use jar lifter to carefully remove jars, without tilting, and place on a towel.

10 Let jars cool, undisturbed, for 12 to 24 hours. Once completely cool, test the seals by gently pressing down on the center of the lids—they should not flex (see page 35).

# BLACKBERRY PRESERVES

SUMMER | WATER BATH | YIELD: 7 (8-OZ) HALF-PINT JARS

*Rich and flavorful, these blackberry preserves highlight the deep, tart sweetness of ripe berries. Their natural pectin ensures a perfect consistency.*

### INGREDIENTS

6 cups fresh blackberries
(approx. 3½ pounds), gently crushed

¼ cup bottled lemon juice

3 tbsp powdered pectin

5 cups granulated sugar

### INSTRUCTIONS

1   Fill your water canner roughly three-quarters full of water. Bring to a boil over high heat.

2   Prepare jars, bands, and lids for canning and keep warm (see page 33).

3   In a large, deep saucepan, combine crushed blackberries, lemon juice, and pectin. Bring to a full boil over medium-high heat, stirring constantly to prevent sticking.

4   Carefully add all of the sugar. Stirring constantly, return the mixture to a rolling boil. Boil hard for 1 minute. Test for doneness using the cold plate or spoon test (see page 59). Using a slotted spoon, skim off any foam that forms on the surface. Turn off heat.

5   Ladle the hot preserves into prepared jars, leaving ¼-inch headspace. Remove bubbles using a bubble remover (see page 34).

6   Using a clean, damp cloth or paper towel, wipe rims clean. Place sterilized lids on jars. Then screw on bands and tighten just until fingertip-tight (see page 34).

7   Using a jar lifter, place jars in canner rack. Submerge rack in boiling water, ensuring jars are covered by at least 1 inch of water (see page 34). Cover canner with lid and bring water to a rolling boil.

8   Process jars for 10 minutes (adjust for altitude, if needed; see page 198). At end of processing time, turn off heat and remove lid.

9   Once water has stopped boiling, use jar lifter to carefully remove jars, without tilting, and place on a towel.

10  Let jars cool, undisturbed, for 12 to 24 hours. Once completely cool, test the seals by gently pressing down on the center of the lids—they should not flex (see page 35).

# CHERRY PRESERVES
## SUMMER | WATER BATH | YIELD: 7 (8-OZ) HALF-PINT JARS

*Juicy, sweet cherries shine in this simple yet flavorful preserve—perfect for toast, pastries, or pairing with cheese.*

### INGREDIENTS

6 cups pitted and halved fresh cherries

4 tbsp bottled lemon juice

2 tbsp powdered pectin

5 cups granulated sugar

### INSTRUCTIONS

1   Fill your water canner roughly three-quarters full of water. Bring to a boil over high heat.

2   Prepare jars, bands, and lids for canning and keep warm (see page 33).

3   In a large, deep saucepan, combine cherries, lemon juice, and pectin. Bring to a full boil over high heat, stirring constantly to prevent sticking.

4   Carefully add all of the sugar. Stirring constantly, return the mixture to a rolling boil. Boil hard for 1 minute. Test for doneness using the cold plate or spoon test (see page 59). Using a slotted spoon, skim off any foam that forms on the surface. Turn off heat.

5   Ladle the hot preserves into prepared jars, leaving ¼-inch headspace. Remove bubbles using a bubble remover (see page 34).

6   Using a clean, damp cloth or paper towel, wipe rims clean. Place sterilized lids on jars. Then screw on bands and tighten just until fingertip-tight (see page 34).

7   Using a jar lifter, place jars in canner rack. Submerge rack in boiling water, ensuring jars are covered by at least 1 inch of water (see page 34). Cover canner with lid and bring water to a rolling boil.

8   Process jars for 10 minutes (adjust for altitude, if needed; see page 198). At end of processing time, turn off heat and remove lid.

9   Once water has stopped boiling, use jar lifter to carefully remove jars, without tilting, and place on a towel.

10  Let jars cool, undisturbed, for 12 to 24 hours. Once completely cool, test the seals by gently pressing down on the center of the lids—they should not flex (see page 35).

# PLUM JAM

## LATE SUMMER | WATER BATH | YIELD: 7 (8-OZ) HALF-PINT JARS

*For this plum jam, I like to use a mix of red and yellow plums for a balance of sweet and tart flavors. If you've never worked with plums before, don't be tempted to peel them—the skins dissolve beautifully into the jam, adding depth of flavor and a rich, ruby hue. If your plums are especially ripe, you may need a little extra pectin to ensure a good set, but don't stress too much—imperfect jam still makes for perfect spoonfuls over yogurt, biscuits, or even a warm bowl of oatmeal on a cold morning.*

### INGREDIENTS

6 cups pitted and chopped plums
(approx. 4 pounds)

¼ cup bottled lemon juice

3 tbsp powdered pectin

5 cups granulated sugar

### INSTRUCTIONS

1   Fill your water canner roughly three-quarters full of water. Bring to a boil over high heat.

2   Prepare jars, bands, and lids for canning and keep warm (see page 33).

3   In a large, deep saucepan, combine chopped plums, lemon juice, and pectin. Bring to a full boil over high heat, stirring constantly to prevent sticking.

4   Carefully add all of the sugar. Stirring constantly, return the mixture to a rolling boil. Boil hard for 1 minute. Test for doneness using the cold plate or spoon test (see page 59). Using a slotted spoon, skim off any foam that forms on the surface. Turn off heat.

5   Ladle the hot jam into prepared jars, leaving ¼-inch headspace. Remove bubbles using a bubble remover (see page 34).

6   Using a clean, damp cloth or paper towel, wipe rims clean. Place sterilized lids on jars. Then screw on bands and tighten just until fingertip-tight (see page 34).

7   Using a jar lifter, place jars in canner rack. Submerge rack in boiling water, ensuring jars are covered by at least 1 inch of water (see page 34). Cover canner with lid and bring water to a rolling boil.

8   Process jars for 15 minutes (adjust for altitude, if needed; see page 198). At end of processing time, turn off heat and remove lid.

9   Once water has stopped boiling, use jar lifter to carefully remove jars, without tilting, and place on a towel.

10   Let jars cool, undisturbed, for 12 to 24 hours. Once completely cool, test the seals by gently pressing down on the center of the lids—they should not flex (see page 35).

# RASPBERRY JAM

SUMMER | WATER BATH | YIELD: 8 (8-OZ) HALF-PINT JARS

*This raspberry jam strikes a perfect balance between tart and sweet, making it a staple for breakfast spreads or pastries, or even as a glaze for roasted meats.*

### INGREDIENTS

6 cups fresh raspberries
(approx. 3 pounds), gently crushed

4 tbsp bottled lemon juice

3 tbsp powdered pectin

5 cups granulated sugar

### INSTRUCTIONS

1   Fill your water canner roughly three-quarters full of water. Bring to a boil over high heat.

2   Prepare jars, bands, and lids for canning and keep warm (see page 33).

3   In a large, deep saucepan, combine crushed raspberries, lemon juice, and pectin. Bring to a full boil over medium-high heat, stirring constantly to prevent sticking.

4   Carefully add all of the sugar. Stirring constantly, return the mixture to a rolling boil. Boil hard for 1 minute. Test for doneness using the cold plate or spoon test (see page 59). Using a slotted spoon, skim off any foam that forms on the surface. Turn off heat.

5   Ladle the hot jam into prepared jars, leaving ¼-inch headspace. Remove bubbles using a bubble remover (see page 34).

6   Using a clean, damp cloth or paper towel, wipe rims clean. Place sterilized lids on jars. Then screw on bands and tighten just until fingertip-tight (see page 34).

7   Using a jar lifter, place jars in canner rack. Submerge rack in boiling water, ensuring jars are covered by at least 1 inch of water (see page 34). Cover canner with lid and bring water to a rolling boil.

8   Process jars for 10 minutes (adjust for altitude, if needed; see page 198). At end of processing time, turn off heat and remove lid.

9   Once water has stopped boiling, use jar lifter to carefully remove jars, without tilting, and place on a towel.

10  Let jars cool, undisturbed, for 12 to 24 hours. Once completely cool, test the seals by gently pressing down on the center of the lids—they should not flex (see page 35).

# GRAPE JELLY

FALL | WATER BATH | YIELD: 8 (8-OZ) HALF-PINT JARS

*There's something timeless about a jar of deep-purple Concord grape jelly—its sweet, tangy flavor feels like pure nostalgia. While Concord grapes provide the deepest, richest flavor, this recipe works just as well with a blend of different grape varieties. No fresh grapes? No problem! You can use pure, unsweetened store-bought grape juice instead of juicing your own—the results will still be delicious.*

## INGREDIENTS

4 cups fresh grape juice (from approx. 5 pounds Concord grapes, or use pure, unsweetened store-bought grape juice)

2 tbsp bottled lemon juice

3 tbsp powdered pectin

3 cups granulated sugar

## INSTRUCTIONS

1   Fill your water canner roughly three-quarters full of water. Bring to a boil over high heat.

2   Prepare jars, bands, and lids for canning and keep warm (see page 33).

3   In a large, deep saucepan, combine grape juice, lemon juice, and pectin. Bring to a full boil over high heat, stirring constantly to prevent sticking.

4   Carefully add all of the sugar. Stirring constantly, return the mixture to a rolling boil. Boil hard for 1 minute. Test for doneness using the cold plate or spoon test (see page 59). Using a slotted spoon, skim off any foam that forms on the surface. Turn off heat.

5   Ladle the hot jelly into prepared jars, leaving ¼-inch headspace. Remove bubbles using a bubble remover (see page 34).

6   Using a clean, damp cloth or paper towel, wipe rims clean. Place sterilized lids on jars. Then screw on bands and tighten just until fingertip-tight (see page 34).

7   Using a jar lifter, place jars in canner rack. Submerge rack in boiling water, ensuring jars are covered by at least 1 inch of water (see page 34). Cover canner with lid and bring water to a rolling boil.

8   Process jars for 10 minutes (adjust for altitude, if needed; see page 198). At end of processing time, turn off heat and remove lid.

9   Once water has stopped boiling, use jar lifter to carefully remove jars, without tilting, and place on a towel.

10  Let jars cool, undisturbed, for 12 to 24 hours. Once completely cool, test the seals by gently pressing down on the center of the lids—they should not flex (see page 35).

# APPLE BUTTER

FALL | WATER BATH | YIELD: 8 (8-OZ) HALF-PINT JARS

*Nothing says fall quite like the deep, caramelized sweetness of homemade apple butter. Simmered low and slow until thick and velvety, this spreadable treat is a cold-weather essential—I like to keep a jar on hand for impromptu visitors, serving it alongside biscuits and sharp cheddar cheese. This version is lightly spiced for warmth, but you can easily customize it with bolder flavors like chai, maple, or rum (see Variations). Using a slow cooker makes the process even easier (see Tip).*

### INGREDIENTS

6 pounds apples, peeled, cored, and chopped

¼ cup bottled lemon juice

1 cup granulated sugar (adjust based on apple sweetness)

½ cup packed brown sugar

1 tbsp ground cinnamon

1 tsp ground nutmeg

1 tsp ground cloves

### INSTRUCTIONS

1 Fill your water canner roughly three-quarters full of water. Bring to a boil over high heat.

2 Prepare jars, bands, and lids for canning and keep warm (see page 33).

3 Cook apples: In a large, deep saucepan, combine chopped apples and lemon juice. Cook over medium heat, stirring occasionally, until the apples are very soft (20 to 30 minutes). (For slow cooker method, see Tip.)

4 Using an immersion blender or potato masher, blend or mash the softened apples until smooth.

5 Stir in granulated sugar, brown sugar, cinnamon, nutmeg, and cloves.

6 Reduce heat to very low and simmer, stirring occasionally, for 2 to 4 hours, until the apple butter darkens and thickens. It should reach 220°F on a candy thermometer and should mound on a spoon without running.

7 Ladle the hot apple butter into prepared jars, leaving ¼-inch headspace. Remove bubbles using a bubble remover (see page 34).

8 Using a clean, damp cloth or paper towel, wipe rims clean. Place sterilized lids on jars. Then screw on bands and tighten just until fingertip-tight (see page 34).

9 Using a jar lifter, place jars in canner rack. Submerge rack in boiling water, ensuring jars are covered by at least 1 inch of water (see page 34). Cover canner with lid and bring water to a rolling boil.

10 Process jars for 15 minutes (adjust for altitude, if needed; see page 198). At end of processing time, turn off heat and remove lid.

11 Once water has stopped boiling, use jar lifter to carefully remove jars, without tilting, and place on a towel.

12 Let jars cool, undisturbed, for 12 to 24 hours. Once completely cool, test the seals by gently pressing down on the center of the lids—they should not flex (see page 35).

## TIP

Using a slow cooker makes this recipe no-fuss. Add the chopped apples and lemon juice to a slow cooker. Cover and cook on low for 8 to 10 hours, stirring occasionally. Once the apples are soft, blend with an immersion blender or mash until smooth. Stir in the sugars and spices, then cook, uncovered, on low for another 4 to 6 hours, stirring occasionally, until thickened and spreadable. Proceed with canning as directed.

## VARIATIONS

**Chai-Spiced Apple Butter:** In Step 5, add 1 tsp ground cardamom and 1 tsp ground ginger along with the other spices.

**Maple Apple Butter:** In Step 5, replace half of the granulated sugar with ½ cup pure maple syrup.

**Rum Apple Butter:** In Step 6, stir in 2 tbsp dark rum during the last 5 minutes of cooking, just before reaching the gel stage.

# ORANGE MARMALADE
## WINTER | WATER BATH | YIELD: 7 (8-OZ) HALF-PINT JARS

*There's something deeply comforting about a jar of homemade orange marmalade. The process is as old-fashioned as it gets—slow-simmering citrus, coaxing out both its bright acidity and natural sweetness, until you're left with a golden preserve that glows like winter sunshine. This perfectly balanced marmalade has the right mix of sweet and bitter, but if you're feeling adventurous, try infusing it with rosemary for an herbal twist or adding a splash of whiskey for a sophisticated depth of flavor (see Variations).*

### INGREDIENTS

2 large oranges (approx. 1½ pounds), peeled, flesh reserved

1 lemon

6 cups water

6 cups granulated sugar

### INSTRUCTIONS

1   Fill your water canner roughly three-quarters full of water. Bring to a boil over high heat.

2   Prepare jars, bands, and lids for canning and keep warm (see page 33).

3   Using a sharp knife, cut the orange peels into thin strips (approx. ⅛ inch thick) and set aside. If preferred, scrape off excess pith before slicing to reduce bitterness. Seed the oranges and discard any tough membranes, reserving only the flesh.

4   Place the peels in a saucepan of water and boil for 5 minutes. Drain and repeat once or twice to reduce bitterness.

5   In a large, deep saucepan, combine blanched peels, reserved citrus flesh, juice of 1 lemon, and water.

6   Carefully add all of the sugar. Increase heat to medium-high and cook, stirring continuously, until the marmalade reaches gel stage (220°F on a candy thermometer; see Tip).

7   Ladle the hot marmalade into prepared jars, leaving ¼-inch headspace. Remove bubbles using a bubble remover (see page 34).

8   Using a clean, damp cloth or paper towel, wipe rims clean. Place sterilized lids on jars. Then screw on bands and tighten just until fingertip-tight (see page 34).

9   Using a jar lifter, place jars in canner rack. Submerge rack in boiling water, ensuring jars are covered by at least 1 inch of water (see page 34). Cover canner with lid and bring water to a rolling boil.

10   Process jars for 10 minutes (adjust for altitude, if needed; see page 198). At end of processing time, turn off heat and remove lid.

11 Once water has stopped boiling, use jar lifter to carefully remove jars, without tilting, and place on a towel.

12 Let jars cool, undisturbed, for 12 to 24 hours. Once completely cool, test the seals by gently pressing down on the center of the lids—they should not flex (see page 35).

---

**TIP**

To test if the marmalade has reached the correct consistency, drop a small amount onto a chilled plate. If it wrinkles when pushed, it's ready to be jarred.

---

**VARIATIONS**

**Orange Rosemary Marmalade:** In Step 5, add 1 tbsp finely chopped fresh rosemary while simmering the citrus mixture.

**Spiced Orange Marmalade:** In Step 5, add 1 tsp ground cinnamon and ¼ tsp ground cloves while simmering the citrus mixture.

**Whiskey Orange Marmalade:** In Step 7, just before ladling into jars, stir in ¼ cup whiskey.

# LOW-SUGAR BERRY PRESERVES

SUMMER | WATER BATH | YIELD: 6 (8-OZ) HALF-PINT JARS

*This recipe delivers a delicious blend of fresh mixed berries with reduced sugar, allowing the natural flavors of the fruit to shine. Designed for those who prefer less sweetness or want something a bit more fruit-forward, these preserves are perfect for breakfast spreads, desserts, or swirling into yogurt. Unlike traditional high-sugar jams, this version relies on low-sugar pectin to create the right consistency without excessive sweetness.*

## INGREDIENTS

4 cups fresh mixed berries (e.g., blackberries, raspberries, and blueberries), gently crushed

2 tbsp bottled lemon juice

2 tbsp low-sugar or no-sugar powdered pectin

½ cup granulated sugar

## INSTRUCTIONS

1   Fill your water canner roughly three-quarters full of water. Bring to a boil over high heat.

2   Prepare jars, bands, and lids for canning and keep warm (see page 33).

3   In a large, deep saucepan, combine crushed berries, lemon juice, and pectin.

4   Bring the mixture to a full boil over medium-high heat, stirring constantly to prevent sticking.

5   Carefully add all of the sugar. Stirring constantly, return the mixture to a rolling boil. Boil hard for 1 minute. Test for doneness using the cold plate or spoon test (see page 59). Using a slotted spoon, skim off any foam that forms on the surface. Turn off heat.

6   Ladle the hot jam into prepared jars, leaving ¼-inch headspace. Remove bubbles using a bubble remover (see page 34).

7   Using a clean, damp cloth or paper towel, wipe rims clean. Place sterilized lids on jars. Then screw on bands and tighten just until fingertip-tight (see page 34).

8   Using a jar lifter, place jars in canner rack. Submerge rack in boiling water, ensuring jars are covered by at least 1 inch of water (see page 34). Cover canner with lid and bring water to a rolling boil.

9   Process jars for 10 minutes (adjust for altitude, if needed; see page 198). At end of processing time, turn off heat and remove lid.

10  Once water has stopped boiling, use jar lifter to carefully remove jars, without tilting, and place on a towel.

11  Let jars cool, undisturbed, for 12 to 24 hours. Once completely cool, test the seals by gently pressing down on the center of the lids—they should not flex (see page 35).

# NECTARINE JAM

SUMMER | WATER BATH | YIELD: 6 (8-OZ) HALF-PINT JARS

*This bright and juicy nectarine jam captures the essence of summer in every spoonful. Whether slathered on warm biscuits, drizzled over yogurt, or used as a glaze for roasted meats, its balance of sweetness and acidity makes it incredibly versatile. Unlike peaches, nectarines have smooth skins, making them easy to work with—though blanching can help remove the skins for a smoother-textured jam.*

## INGREDIENTS

4 cups peeled, pitted, and chopped (¼- to ½-inch pieces) nectarines (approx. 6 medium nectarines)

2 tbsp bottled lemon juice

2 tbsp powdered pectin

3 cups granulated sugar

## INSTRUCTIONS

1   Fill your water canner roughly three-quarters full of water. Bring to a boil over high heat.

2   Prepare jars, bands, and lids for canning and keep warm (see page 33).

3   In a large, deep saucepan, combine chopped nectarines, lemon juice, and pectin. Bring the mixture to a full boil over high heat, stirring constantly to prevent sticking.

4   Carefully add all of the sugar. Stirring constantly, return the mixture to a rolling boil. Boil hard for 1 minute. Test for doneness using the cold plate or spoon test (see page 59). Using a slotted spoon, skim off any foam that forms on the surface. Turn off heat.

5   Ladle the hot jam into prepared jars, leaving ¼-inch headspace. Remove bubbles using a bubble remover (see page 34).

6   Using a clean, damp cloth or paper towel, wipe rims clean. Place sterilized lids on jars. Then screw on bands and tighten just until fingertip-tight (see page 34).

7   Using a jar lifter, place jars in canner rack. Submerge rack in boiling water, ensuring jars are covered by at least 1 inch of water (see page 34). Cover canner with lid and bring water to a rolling boil.

8   Process jars for 10 minutes (adjust for altitude, if needed; see page 198). At end of processing time, turn off heat and remove lid.

9   Once water has stopped boiling, use jar lifter to carefully remove jars, without tilting, and place on a towel.

10  Let jars cool, undisturbed, for 12 to 24 hours. Once completely cool, test the seals by gently pressing down on the center of the lids—they should not flex (see page 35).

# HONEY-SWEETENED BERRY JAM

SUMMER | WATER BATH | YIELD: 6 (8-OZ) HALF-PINT JARS

*With a smooth consistency and a balanced sweetness, thanks to honey, this vibrant mixed-berry jam is an excellent choice for those looking to reduce refined sugar while still preserving the season's bounty. The honey enhances the berries' natural flavors without overpowering them.*

## INGREDIENTS

4 cups fresh mixed berries (e.g., blueberries, raspberries, and strawberries), crushed

1 cup liquid honey (mild flavor, such as clover or wildflower)

2 tbsp bottled lemon juice

2 tbsp powdered pectin

## INSTRUCTIONS

1  Fill your water canner roughly three-quarters full of water. Bring to a boil over high heat.

2  Prepare jars, bands, and lids for canning and keep warm (see page 33).

3  In a large, deep saucepan, combine crushed berries, honey, lemon juice, and pectin. Bring to a full boil over medium-high heat, stirring constantly to prevent sticking.

4  Boil hard for 1 minute. Test for doneness using the cold plate or spoon test (see page 59). Using a slotted spoon, skim off any foam that forms on the surface. Turn off heat.

5  Ladle the hot jam into prepared jars, leaving ¼-inch headspace. Remove bubbles using a bubble remover (see page 34).

6  Using a clean, damp cloth or paper towel, wipe rims clean. Place sterilized lids on jars. Then screw on bands and tighten just until fingertip-tight (see page 34).

7  Using a jar lifter, place jars in canner rack. Submerge rack in boiling water, ensuring jars are covered by at least 1 inch of water (see page 34). Cover canner with the lid and bring water to a rolling boil.

8  Process jars for 10 minutes (adjust for altitude, if needed; see page 198). At end of processing time, turn off heat and remove lid.

9  Once water has stopped boiling, use jar lifter to carefully remove jars, without tilting, and place on a towel.

10  Let jars cool, undisturbed, for 12 to 24 hours. Once completely cool, test the seals by gently pressing down on the center of the lids—they should not flex (see page 35).

# PINEAPPLE JALAPEÑO JELLY

**SUMMER | WATER BATH | YIELD: 6 (8-OZ) HALF-PINT JARS**

*This sweet-and-spicy jelly balances the tropical brightness of fresh pineapple with the gentle heat of jalapeño, creating a versatile condiment with a kick. Spread it over cream cheese and crackers; use it as a glaze for grilled shrimp, pork, or chicken; or slather it onto sandwiches and burgers for a burst of bold flavor.*

## INGREDIENTS

4 cups crushed fresh pineapple
(approx. 1 medium pineapple)

2 fresh jalapeños, seeded and finely chopped

4 tbsp bottled lemon juice

3 tbsp powdered pectin

3 cups granulated sugar

## INSTRUCTIONS

1   Fill your water canner roughly three-quarters full of water. Bring to a boil over high heat.

2   Prepare jars, bands, and lids for canning and keep warm (see page 33).

3   In a large, deep saucepan, combine crushed pineapple, jalapeños, lemon juice, and pectin. Stir well to combine. Bring the mixture to a rolling boil over medium-high heat, stirring constantly to prevent scorching.

4   Carefully add all of the sugar. Stirring constantly, return the mixture to a rolling boil. Boil hard for 1 minute. Test for doneness using the cold plate or spoon test (see page 59). Using a slotted spoon, skim off any foam that forms on the surface. Turn off heat.

5   Ladle the hot jelly into prepared jars, leaving ¼-inch headspace. Remove bubbles using a bubble remover (see page 34).

6   Using a clean, damp cloth or paper towel, wipe rims clean. Place sterilized lids on jars. Then screw on bands and tighten just until fingertip-tight (see page 34).

7   Using a jar lifter, place jars in canner rack. Submerge rack in boiling water, ensuring jars are covered by at least 1 inch of water (see page 34). Cover canner with the lid and bring water to a rolling boil.

8   Process jars for 10 minutes (adjust for altitude, if needed; see page 198). At end of processing time, turn off heat and remove lid.

9   Once water has stopped boiling, use jar lifter to carefully remove jars, without tilting, and place on a towel.

10  Let jars cool, undisturbed, for 12 to 24 hours. Once completely cool, test the seals by gently pressing down on the center of the lids—they should not flex (see page 35).

# FIG AND ORANGE CONSERVE

**FALL/WINTER | WATER BATH | YIELD: 5 (8-OZ) HALF-PINT JARS**

*Unlike jams, which are made with fresh fruit, conserves feature a blend of dried and fresh ingredients, making them perfect for pairing with cheese boards, yogurt, toast, or roasted meats. This conserve combines the deep, natural sweetness of dried figs with bright, citrusy orange, resulting in a well-balanced spread with a complex flavor.*

## INGREDIENTS

2 cups chopped dried figs (approx. 8 ounces)

Zest of 1 orange

1 cup orange juice (fresh or bottled, 100% juice)

2 cups granulated sugar

## INSTRUCTIONS

1   Fill your water canner roughly three-quarters full of water. Bring to a boil over high heat.

2   Prepare jars, bands, and lids for canning and keep warm (see page 33).

3   In a large, deep saucepan, combine chopped figs, orange zest, orange juice, and sugar.

4   Heat over medium-high heat, stirring frequently, until the mixture comes to a boil. Reduce heat and simmer for 20 to 25 minutes, stirring occasionally, until the conserve thickens.

5   Ladle the hot conserve into prepared jars, leaving ¼-inch headspace. Remove bubbles using a bubble remover (see page 34).

6   Using a clean, damp cloth or paper towel, wipe rims clean. Place sterilized lids on jars. Then screw on bands and tighten just until fingertip-tight (see page 34).

7   Using a jar lifter, place jars in canner rack. Submerge rack in boiling water, ensuring jars are covered by at least 1 inch of water (see page 34). Cover canner with the lid and bring water to a rolling boil.

8   Process jars for 10 minutes (adjust for altitude, if needed; see page 198). At end of processing time, turn off heat and remove lid.

9   Once water has stopped boiling, use jar lifter to carefully remove jars, without tilting, and place on a towel.

10  Let jars cool, undisturbed, for 12 to 24 hours. Once completely cool, test the seals by gently pressing down on the center of the lids—they should not flex (see page 35).

# MANGO LIME BUTTER

## SUMMER | WATER BATH | YIELD: 5 (8-OZ) HALF-PINT JARS

*Smooth, creamy, and bursting with tropical flavor, Mango Lime Butter is a luscious spread perfect for scones, crepes, or yogurt, or even as a cake filling. Naturally sweet and vibrant, this fruit butter is a summer staple for any pantry.*

### INGREDIENTS

4 cups puréed fresh mango
(approx. 3 large mangoes)

¼ cup bottled lime juice

2 tbsp powdered pectin

3 cups granulated sugar

### INSTRUCTIONS

1   Fill your water canner roughly three-quarters full of water. Bring to a boil over high heat.

2   Prepare jars, bands, and lids for canning and keep warm (see page 33).

3   In a large, deep saucepan, combine mango purée, lime juice, and powdered pectin. Stir well to dissolve the pectin. Bring the mixture to a rolling boil over medium-high heat, stirring frequently to prevent sticking.

4   Carefully add all of the sugar. Stirring constantly, return the mixture to a rolling boil. Boil hard for 1 minute. Test for doneness using the cold plate or spoon test (see page 59). Using a slotted spoon, skim off any foam that forms on the surface. Turn off heat.

5   Ladle the hot mango butter into prepared jars, leaving ¼-inch headspace. Remove bubbles using a bubble remover (see page 34).

6   Using a clean, damp cloth or paper towel, wipe rims clean. Place sterilized lids on jars. Then screw on bands and tighten just until fingertip-tight (see page 34).

7   Using a jar lifter, place jars in canner rack. Submerge rack in boiling water, ensuring jars are covered by at least 1 inch of water (see page 34). Cover canner with the lid and bring water to a rolling boil.

8   Process jars for 10 minutes (adjust for altitude, if needed; see page 198). At end of processing time, turn off heat and remove lid.

9   Once water has stopped boiling, use jar lifter to carefully remove jars, without tilting, and place on a towel.

10  Let jars cool, undisturbed, for 12 to 24 hours. Once completely cool, test the seals by gently pressing down on the center of the lids—they should not flex (see page 35).

# CHAPTER 6

# VEGETABLES

**WATER BATH CANNING**

| | |
|---|---|
| Whole Tomatoes | 80 |
| Zucchini Relish | 81 |
| Pickled Bell Peppers | 82 |
| Pickled Carrots | 84 |
| Pickled Asparagus | 85 |
| Pickled Vegetable Medley | 86 |
| Classic Dill Pickles | 88 |
| Bread-and-Butter Pickles | 90 |
| Sweet Pickled Gherkins | 92 |
| Pickled Dilly Beans | 94 |
| Mixed Vegetable Pickle | 95 |
| Mixed Garden Pickle | 96 |
| Sweet Relish | 97 |
| Corn Relish | 98 |

**PRESSURE CANNING**

| | |
|---|---|
| Potatoes | 99 |
| Carrots | 100 |
| Mixed Vegetables | 102 |
| Pumpkin | 104 |
| Corn | 106 |
| Sweet Potatoes | 108 |
| Winter Squash | 109 |
| Mixed Braising Greens | 110 |
| Mushrooms | 112 |

## PICKLE PERFECTION

Nothing beats the tangy crunch of homemade pickles, and achieving the perfect balance of flavor, texture, and preservation is easier than you think! Whether you're making classic cucumber pickles, spicy dilly beans, or crisp pickled carrots, understanding the fundamentals of vegetable selection, brine ratios, and processing techniques ensures success. Follow these guidelines to master the art of pickling, and enjoy your favorite preserved vegetables all year long.

## VEGETABLE SELECTION

Begin with fresh, high-quality vegetables to ensure the best flavor and texture retention. Cucumbers, green beans, carrots, cauliflower, radishes, and peppers all make excellent choices for pickling. Choose firm, unblemished produce, and avoid overly ripe vegetables, which may become mushy during processing.

## BRINE RATIO

A fundamental brine ratio for safe and well-balanced pickles is:

1 cup vinegar (5% acidity) per 1 cup water

1 tbsp pickling salt

This ratio ensures proper acidity for long-term preservation while maintaining great taste. Feel free to customize flavors by adding whole spices, garlic, or fresh herbs, but never reduce the vinegar content below the recommended level.

## TRICKS FOR CRISPNESS

There are a few different ways to achieve that signature crunch of pickled vegetables everyone enjoys.

Trim the blossom ends off cucumbers to remove the enzymes that cause softening.

Tuck a grape leaf, oak leaf, or cherry leaf into your pickling jars. These leaves contain natural tannins that help maintain crispness.

Add a measure of Pickle Crisp (calcium chloride) to each of your jars (follow the directions on the label). Pickle Crisp is an effective modern option that firms up vegetables without altering flavor.

Avoid overprocessing. Excessive heat during water bath canning can soften vegetables.

# WHOLE TOMATOES

## SUMMER | WATER BATH | YIELD: 6 (32-OZ) QUART JARS

*There's nothing quite like opening a jar of home-canned tomatoes in the middle of winter. They are easier to preserve than you think, and are the perfect base for all your favorite meals.*

### INGREDIENTS

21 pounds fresh tomatoes

6 tbsp bottled lemon juice, divided

6 tsp pickling salt, divided (optional)

### INSTRUCTIONS

1 Fill your water canner roughly three-quarters full of water. Bring to a boil over high heat.

2 Prepare jars, bands, and lids for canning and keep warm (see page 33).

3 Peel tomatoes: In a large bowl, prepare an ice bath. Bring a large pot of water to a boil. Meanwhile, using a paring knife, cut a small X on the bottom of each tomato. Add tomatoes to water and boil (blanch) for 30 to 60 seconds. Using a slotted spoon or spider, transfer blanched tomatoes to the ice bath. Peel the skins and cut away any blemished areas.

4 To each jar, add 1 tbsp of the lemon juice and 1 tsp of the salt (if using).

5 Pack the peeled tomatoes tightly into jars, pressing gently to release their juices. Leave ½-inch headspace. Remove bubbles using a bubble remover (see page 34).

6 Using a clean, damp cloth or paper towel, wipe rims clean. Place sterilized lids on jars. Then screw on bands and tighten just until fingertip-tight (see page 34).

7 Using a jar lifter, place jars in canner rack. Submerge rack in boiling water, ensuring jars are covered by at least 1 inch of water. (You may need to add a little extra boiling water.) Cover canner with lid and bring water to a rolling boil.

8 Process jars for 45 minutes (adjust for altitude, if needed; see page 198). At end of processing time, turn off heat and remove lid.

9 Once water has stopped boiling, use jar lifter to carefully remove jars, without tilting, and place on a towel.

10 Let jars cool, undisturbed, for 12 to 24 hours. Once completely cool, test the seals by gently pressing down on the center of the lids—they should not flex (see page 35).

# ZUCCHINI RELISH

SUMMER | WATER BATH | YIELD: 6 (16-OZ) PINT JARS

*This zucchini relish is a flavorful, slightly sweet twist on classic relish. It's an excellent way to use up excess summer zucchini and adds a vibrant, tangy touch to sandwiches, grilled meats, and salads.*

## INGREDIENTS

6 cups grated zucchini
(approx. 3 or 4 medium zucchini)

2 cups finely chopped yellow or white onions

1 cup finely chopped red bell pepper

1 cup finely chopped green bell pepper

¼ cup pickling salt

3 cups pickling vinegar (5% acidity)

1½ cups granulated sugar

1 tbsp mustard seeds

1 tsp celery seeds

½ tsp ground turmeric

## INSTRUCTIONS

1   In a large bowl, combine prepared vegetables and salt. Set aside for 2 hours.

2   Transfer vegetables to a colander and rinse well under cool running water.

3   Fill your water canner roughly three-quarters full of water. Bring to a boil over high heat.

4   Prepare jars, bands, and lids for canning and keep warm (see page 33).

5   Make brine: In a large pot, combine vinegar, sugar, mustard seeds, celery seeds, and turmeric and bring to a boil. Heat, stirring occasionally, until the sugar has completely dissolved.

6   Add drained vegetables to the brine. Simmer for 10 minutes, stirring occasionally.

7   Ladle the hot relish into prepared jars, leaving ½-inch headspace. Remove bubbles using a bubble remover (see page 34).

8   Using a clean, damp cloth or paper towel, wipe rims clean. Place sterilized lids on jars. Then screw on bands and tighten just until fingertip-tight (see page 34).

9   Using a jar lifter, place jars in canner rack. Submerge rack in boiling water, ensuring jars are covered by at least 1 inch of water. (You may need to add a little extra boiling water.) Cover canner with lid and bring water to a rolling boil.

10  Process jars for 15 minutes (adjust for altitude, if needed; see page 198). At end of processing time, turn off heat and remove lid.

11  Once water has stopped boiling, use jar lifter to carefully remove jars, without tilting, and place on a towel.

12  Let jars cool, undisturbed, for 12 to 24 hours. Once completely cool, test the seals by gently pressing down on the center of the lids—they should not flex (see page 35).

# PICKLED BELL PEPPERS

### LATE SUMMER | WATER BATH | YIELD: 6 (16-OZ) PINT JARS

*Bright and colorful, these canned pickled peppers add vibrant flavor to salads, stir-fries, and casseroles. This simple canning method preserves their crisp texture and sweet taste for year-round enjoyment. While bell peppers are naturally delicious on their own, they also provide the perfect canvas for flavor experimentation.*

## INGREDIENTS

3 pounds mixed-color bell peppers, seeded and cut into strips or chunks (see Tips)

2 cups apple cider vinegar (5% acidity)

1 cup water

6 tbsp bottled lemon juice

3 tbsp granulated sugar

6 tsp pickling salt (optional)

2 tsp whole black peppercorns, divided (optional)

6 cloves garlic, divided (optional)

2 tsp dried oregano or basil, divided (optional)

1 tsp crushed red pepper flakes, divided (optional)

## INSTRUCTIONS

1   Fill your water bath canner halfway up the pot. Bring to a simmer.

2   Prepare jars, bands, and lids for canning and keep warm (see page 33).

3   Prepare bell peppers: In a large bowl, prepare an ice bath. Bring a large pot of water to a boil. Add prepared peppers to water and boil (blanch) for 2 minutes. Using a slotted spoon or spider, transfer blanched peppers to the ice bath.

4   Make brine: In a large saucepan, combine apple cider vinegar, water, lemon juice, sugar, and salt (if using). Bring the mixture to a boil, stirring until the sugar and salt have completely dissolved.

5   If using, divide the herbs and spices equally among jars.

6   Pack the blanched pepper strips tightly into jars, pressing gently to release their juices. Leave ½-inch headspace.

7   Pour boiling liquid over the peppers, maintaining ½-inch headspace. Remove bubbles using a bubble remover (see page 34).

8   Using a clean, damp cloth or paper towel, wipe rims clean. Place sterilized lids on jars. Then screw on bands and tighten just until fingertip-tight (see page 34).

9   Using a jar lifter, place jars in canner rack. Submerge rack in boiling water, ensuring jars are covered by at least 1 inch of water. (You may need to add a little extra boiling water.) Cover canner with lid and bring water to a rolling boil.

10　Process jars for 10 minutes (adjust for altitude, if needed; see page 198). At end of processing time, turn off heat and remove lid.

11　Once water has stopped boiling, use jar lifter to carefully remove jars, without tilting, and place on a towel.

12　Let jars cool, undisturbed, for 12 to 24 hours. Once completely cool, test the seals by gently pressing down on the center of the lids—they should not flex (see page 35).

---

**TIPS**

Blanching peppers before canning removes excess air from their cellular structure, preventing floating peppers. It also stops the cooking process and maintains color and texture.

Bell peppers shrink during processing so pack them in firmly while leaving room for liquid circulation.

# PICKLED CARROTS
**SPRING/FALL | WATER BATH | YIELD: 6 (16-OZ) PINT JARS**

*It's hard not to be obsessed with these pickled carrots. They're so tangy and crunchy, you're going to snack on these every time you open the fridge.*

## INGREDIENTS

5 cups pickling vinegar (5% acidity)

1 cup water

4 tsp pickling salt

4 tsp granulated sugar

3 pounds fresh carrots, peeled, trimmed, and cut into sticks or coins

6 cloves garlic, divided (optional)

2 tsp whole black peppercorns, divided (optional)

## INSTRUCTIONS

1 Fill your water canner roughly three-quarters full of water. Bring to a boil over high heat.

2 Prepare jars, bands, and lids for canning and keep warm (see page 33).

3 Make brine: In a large saucepan, combine vinegar, water, salt, and sugar. Bring the mixture to a boil, stirring until the sugar and salt have completely dissolved.

4 Place 1 of the garlic cloves (if using) and a few of the peppercorns (if using) in each jar.

5 Pack the prepared carrots tightly into jars. Leave ½-inch headspace.

6 Ladle the hot brine over the carrots, maintaining ½-inch headspace. Remove bubbles using a bubble remover (see page 34).

7 Using a clean, damp cloth or paper towel, wipe rims clean. Place sterilized lids on jars. Then screw on bands and tighten just until fingertip-tight (see page 34).

8 Using a jar lifter, place jars in canner rack. Submerge rack in boiling water, ensuring jars are covered by at least 1 inch of water. (You may need to add a little extra boiling water.) Cover canner with lid and bring water to a rolling boil.

9 Process jars for 15 minutes (adjust for altitude, if needed; see page 198). At end of processing time, turn off heat and remove lid.

10 Once water has stopped boiling, use jar lifter to carefully remove jars, without tilting, and place on a towel.

11 Let jars cool, undisturbed, for 12 to 24 hours. Once completely cool, test the seals by gently pressing down on the center of the lids—they should not flex (see page 35).

# PICKLED ASPARAGUS

## SPRING | WATER BATH | YIELD: 6 (16-OZ) PINT JARS

*Crisp, tangy pickled asparagus spears are a delicious addition to salads, charcuterie boards, or cocktails. This simple recipe captures their fresh flavor in a perfectly balanced brine.*

### INGREDIENTS

5 cups pickling vinegar (5% acidity)

1 cup water

4 tsp pickling salt

6 cloves garlic, divided

6 sprigs fresh dill, divided

1 tsp red pepper flakes, divided (optional)

3 pounds asparagus, stem trimmed to fit jars

### INSTRUCTIONS

1   Fill your water canner roughly three-quarters full of water. Bring to a boil over high heat.

2   Prepare jars, bands, and lids for canning and keep warm (see page 33).

3   Make brine: In a large saucepan, combine vinegar, water, and salt. Bring the mixture to a boil, stirring until the salt completely dissolves.

4   Place 1 of the garlic cloves, 1 sprig of the dill, and a pinch of the red pepper flakes (if using) in each jar.

5   Pack the prepared asparagus spears tightly into jars. Leave ½-inch headspace.

6   Ladle the hot brine over the asparagus, maintaining ½-inch headspace. Remove bubbles using a bubble remover (see page 34).

7   Using a clean, damp cloth or paper towel, wipe rims clean. Place sterilized lids on jars. Then screw on bands and tighten just until fingertip-tight (see page 34).

8   Using a jar lifter, place jars in canner rack. Submerge rack in boiling water, ensuring jars are covered by at least 1 inch of water. (You may need to add a little extra boiling water.) Cover canner with lid and bring water to a rolling boil.

9   Process jars for 10 minutes (adjust for altitude, if needed; see page 198). At end of processing time, turn off heat and remove lid.

10  Once water has stopped boiling, use jar lifter to carefully remove jars, without tilting, and place on a towel.

11  Let jars cool, undisturbed, for 12 to 24 hours. Once completely cool, test the seals by gently pressing down on the center of the lids—they should not flex (see page 35).

# PICKLED VEGETABLE MEDLEY

SUMMER | WATER BATH | YIELD: 6 (16-OZ) PINT JARS

*Forget store-bought, limp pickled veggies—homemade versions are where it's at. They're fresh, crunchy, and completely customizable. Want a little heat? Add extra red pepper flakes or jalapeños. Love a garlicky kick? Toss in whole cloves. You can even create a Bloody Mary pickle mix by combining carrots, celery, green beans, and pearl onions in the same jar!*

## INGREDIENTS

6 cups pickling vinegar (5% acidity)

2 cups water

4 tsp pickling salt

6 cloves garlic, divided (optional)

1 tsp dried dill, divided (optional)

1 tsp crushed red pepper flakes, divided (optional)

1 tsp mustard seeds

1 tsp celery seeds

1 tsp dill seeds

3 pounds assorted summer vegetables (e.g., pearl onions, cucumbers, carrots, jalapeños, and green beans), cut into bite-size pieces

## INSTRUCTIONS

1 Fill your water canner roughly three-quarters full of water. Bring to a boil over high heat.

2 Prepare jars, bands, and lids for canning and keep warm (see page 33).

3 Make brine: In a large saucepan, combine vinegar, water, and salt. Bring the mixture to a boil, stirring until the salt completely dissolves.

4 Divide the garlic (if using), dried dill (if using), and red pepper flakes (if using), as well as the mustard seeds, celery seeds, and dill seeds, evenly among prepared jars.

5 Pack the prepared vegetables tightly into jars. Leave ½-inch headspace.

6 Ladle the hot brine over the vegetables, maintaining ½-inch headspace. Remove bubbles using a bubble remover (see page 34).

7 Using a clean, damp cloth or paper towel, wipe rims clean. Place sterilized lids on jars. Then screw on bands and tighten just until fingertip-tight (see page 34).

8 Using a jar lifter, place jars in canner rack. Submerge rack in boiling water, ensuring jars are covered by at least 1 inch of water. (You may need to add a little extra boiling water.) Cover canner with lid and bring water to a rolling boil.

9 Process jars for 15 minutes (adjust for altitude, if needed; see page 198). At end of processing time, turn off heat and remove lid.

10  Once water has stopped boiling, use jar lifter to carefully remove jars, without tilting, and place on a towel.

11  Let jars cool, undisturbed, for 12 to 24 hours. Once completely cool, test the seals by gently pressing down on the center of the lids—they should not flex (see page 35).

**TIP**

It may be tempting to add zucchini, but summer squash doesn't hold up well in the canning process, due to excess water (see page 43). A better option would be celery or okra (popular in the South). If you are insistent on using squash, pattypan squash is a good alternative but should be used sparingly.

# CLASSIC DILL PICKLES

**SUMMER | WATER BATH | YIELD: 4 (32-OZ) QUART OR 8 (16-OZ) PINT JARS**

*The first time I made homemade dill pickles, I realized what I had been missing—crisp, tangy perfection, with the perfect balance of garlic, dill, and spice. Now every summer I make batch after batch. Once you've tasted homemade, store-bought will never compare!*

## INGREDIENTS

8 cups water

4 cups pickling vinegar (5% acidity)

½ cup pickling salt

8 heads fresh dill or 4 tsp dill seeds, divided

8 cloves garlic (optional)

4 tsp mustard seeds

2 tsp crushed red pepper flakes (optional)

4 pounds pickling cucumbers (3 to 4 inches long), blossom ends trimmed (see Tip)

## INSTRUCTIONS

1  Fill your water canner roughly three-quarters full of water. Bring to a boil over high heat.

2  Prepare jars, bands, and lids for canning and keep warm (see page 33).

3  Make brine: In a large pot, combine water, vinegar, and salt and bring to a boil, stirring occasionally until the salt has completely dissolved.

4  Meanwhile, divide the dill, garlic (if using), mustard seeds, and red pepper flakes (if using) evenly among prepared jars.

5  Pack the prepared cucumbers tightly into jars, ensuring they remain upright, leaving ½-inch headspace.

6  Ladle the hot brine over the cucumbers, maintaining ½-inch headspace. Remove bubbles using a bubble remover (see page 34).

7  Using a clean, damp cloth or paper towel, wipe rims clean. Place sterilized lids on jars. Then screw on bands and tighten just until fingertip-tight (see page 34).

8  Using a jar lifter, place jars in canner rack. Submerge rack in boiling water, ensuring jars are covered by at least 1 inch of water. (You may need to add a little extra boiling water.) Cover canner with lid and bring water to a rolling boil.

9  Process pint jars for 10 minutes or quarts for 15 minutes (adjust for altitude, if needed; see page 198). At end of processing time, turn off heat and remove lid.

10 Once water has stopped boiling, use jar lifter to carefully remove jars, without tilting, and place on a towel.

11  Let jars cool, undisturbed, for 12 to 24 hours. Once completely cool, test the seals by gently pressing down on the center of the lids—they should not flex (see page 35).

---

TIP

For crunchier pickles, trim the blossom ends. The blossom end of a cucumber contains enzymes that soften pickles, leading to a mushy texture. To prevent this, identify the blossom end—it will be the opposite end of the stem. Use a sharp knife to trim off at least $\frac{1}{16}$ inch from the blossom end before pickling. This simple step helps preserve crunch and enhance pickle texture.

Adding Pickle Crisp (calcium chloride) to your jars before filling can help maintain crunch without affecting flavor (follow the label for quantity based on jar size).

# BREAD-AND-BUTTER PICKLES

**SUMMER | WATER BATH | YIELD: 4 (16-OZ) PINT JARS**

*Growing up, I always thought store-bought bread-and-butter pickles were too sweet—until I made my own. The perfect balance of tangy, sweet, and salty, these homemade pickles are incredibly crisp, adding a delicious crunch to sandwiches, salads, and charcuterie boards. The secret to keeping them crisp lies in the presalting process—which helps draw out moisture before cooking—and not overcooking the cucumbers in the brine.*

## INGREDIENTS

6 cups thinly sliced (¼ inch) cucumbers

2 cups thinly sliced white or yellow onions

¼ cup pickling salt

1 cup pickling vinegar (5% acidity)

1 cup apple cider vinegar (5% acidity)

2 cups granulated sugar

1 tbsp mustard seeds

1 tsp celery seeds

½ tsp ground turmeric

## INSTRUCTIONS

1 In a large bowl, gently combine prepared cucumbers, onions, and salt. Let sit for 2 to 3 hours to draw out excess moisture.

2 Fill your water canner roughly three-quarters full of water. Bring to a boil over high heat.

3 Prepare jars, bands, and lids for canning and keep warm (see page 33).

4 Make brine: In a large pot, combine pickling vinegar, apple cider vinegar, sugar, mustard seeds, celery seeds, and turmeric. Bring to a boil, stirring occasionally until the sugar completely dissolves.

5 Transfer cucumber mixture to a colander and rinse under cool running water. Drain well.

6 Add drained cucumber mixture to the brine and simmer for only 5 minutes (this helps to maintain crispness).

7 Using a slotted spoon, pack the cucumbers and onions tightly into prepared jars, leaving ½-inch headspace.

8 Ladle the hot brine over the cucumbers, maintaining ½-inch headspace. Remove bubbles using a bubble remover (see page 34).

9 Using a clean, damp cloth or paper towel, wipe the rims to ensure a proper seal. Place sterilized lids on jars. Then screw on bands and tighten just until fingertip-tight (see page 34).

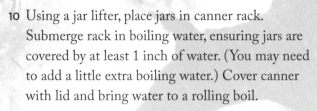

10  Using a jar lifter, place jars in canner rack. Submerge rack in boiling water, ensuring jars are covered by at least 1 inch of water. (You may need to add a little extra boiling water.) Cover canner with lid and bring water to a rolling boil.

11  Process jars for 10 minutes (adjust for altitude, if needed; see page 198). At end of processing time, turn off heat and remove lid.

12  Once water has stopped boiling, use jar lifter to carefully remove jars, without tilting, and place on a towel.

13  Let jars cool, undisturbed, for 12 to 24 hours. Once completely cool, test the seals by gently pressing down on the center of the lids—they should not flex (see page 35).

### TIPS

Use fresh, firm cucumbers (smaller pickling varieties hold their crunch best).

For additional crispness without affecting flavor, add ⅛ tsp Pickle Crisp (calcium chloride) per pint jar.

Avoid overprocessing—excessive heat can soften pickles, so keep processing time precise.

# SWEET PICKLED GHERKINS

## SUMMER | WATER BATH | YIELD: 6 (16-OZ) PINT JARS

*These crisp, sweet gherkins balance tangy and sugary flavors, making them perfect for snacking, sandwiches, or cheese boards. Slice for tea sandwiches, dice into potato salads, or pair with cheese and charcuterie. Note that you'll need to start this recipe a day in advance to allow the cucumbers time to soak in salt water before canning. Their overnight salt soak is key to maintaining that signature crisp texture, so plan ahead and allow time for proper brining.*

### INGREDIENTS

8 cups water, divided

½ cup pickling salt

5 pounds small (1 to 2 inches long) cucumbers

3 cups pickling vinegar (5% acidity)

4 cups granulated sugar

2 tbsp mixed pickling spices

1 tsp ground turmeric

### INSTRUCTIONS

1   Soak cucumbers: In a large container with a lid, combine 4 cups of the water and the salt. Stir until the salt dissolves. Add cucumbers, cover, and refrigerate for 24 hours to improve crispness and flavor.

2   Fill your water canner roughly three-quarters full of water. Bring to a boil over high heat.

3   Prepare jars, bands, and lids for canning and keep warm (see page 33).

4   Make brine: In a large pot, combine remaining 4 cups of water and the vinegar, sugar, pickling spices, and turmeric. Bring to a boil, stirring occasionally until the sugar completely dissolves.

5   Transfer cucumbers to a colander and rinse well under cold running water.

6   Tightly pack the cucumbers into prepared jars, leaving ½-inch headspace.

7   Ladle the hot brine over the cucumbers, maintaining ½-inch headspace. Remove bubbles using a bubble remover (see page 34).

8   Using a clean, damp cloth or paper towel, wipe rims clean. Place sterilized lids on jars. Then screw on bands and tighten just until fingertip-tight (see page 34).

9   Using a jar lifter, place jars in canner rack. Submerge rack in boiling water, ensuring jars are covered by at least 1 inch of water. (You may need to add a little extra boiling water.) Cover canner with lid and bring water to a rolling boil.

10  Process jars for 10 minutes (adjust for altitude, if needed; see page 198). At end of processing time, turn off heat and remove lid.

11 Once water has stopped boiling, use jar lifter to carefully remove jars, without tilting, and place on a towel.

12 Let jars cool, undisturbed, for 12 to 24 hours. Once completely cool, test the seals by gently pressing down on the center of the lids—they should not flex (see page 35).

TIPS

Use fresh, firm cucumbers (smaller pickling varieties hold their crunch best).

For additional crispness without affecting flavor, add ⅛ tsp Pickle Crisp (calcium chloride) per pint jar.

Avoid overprocessing—excessive heat can soften pickles, so keep processing time precise.

# PICKLED DILLY BEANS

SUMMER | WATER BATH | YIELD: 4 (16-OZ) PINT JARS

*Crisp, tangy, and packed with dill flavor, these pickled green beans are perfect for snacking or adding to salads, or as a garnish for cocktails.*

### INGREDIENTS

4 cups water

4 cups pickling vinegar (5% acidity)

½ cup pickling salt

4 cloves garlic, divided

4 tsp dill seeds, divided

2 tsp red pepper flakes, divided (optional)

2 pounds fresh green beans, trimmed to fit jars

### INSTRUCTIONS

1. Fill your water canner roughly three-quarters full of water. Bring to a boil over high heat.

2. Prepare jars, bands, and lids for canning and keep warm (see page 33).

3. Make brine: In a large pot, combine water, vinegar, and salt and bring to a boil. Heat, stirring occasionally, until the salt has completely dissolved.

4. Meanwhile, divide the garlic, dill seeds, and red pepper flakes (if using) evenly among jars.

5. Pack the trimmed beans tightly into prepared jars, leaving ½-inch headspace.

6. Ladle the hot brine over the beans, maintaining ½-inch headspace. Remove bubbles using a bubble remover (see page 34).

7. Using a clean, damp cloth or paper towel, wipe rims clean. Place sterilized lids on jars. Then screw on bands and tighten just until fingertip-tight (see page 34).

8. Using a jar lifter, place jars in canner rack. Submerge rack in boiling water, ensuring jars are covered by at least 1 inch of water. (You may need to add a little extra boiling water.) Cover canner with lid and bring water to a rolling boil.

9. Process jars for 10 minutes (adjust for altitude, if needed; see page 198). At end of processing time, turn off heat and remove lid.

10. Once water has stopped boiling, use jar lifter to carefully remove jars, without tilting, and place on a towel.

11. Let jars cool, undisturbed, for 12 to 24 hours. Once completely cool, test the seals by gently pressing down on the center of the lids—they should not flex (see page 35).

# MIXED VEGETABLE PICKLE

YEAR-ROUND | WATER BATH | YIELD: 6 (16-OZ) PINT JARS

*This tangy, colorful pickle blends crunchy cauliflower, carrots, and celery in a sweet-and-sour brine. Perfect for BBQ sides, antipasto platters, or tacos!*

### INGREDIENTS

2 cups cauliflower florets

2 cups carrot sticks (2- to 3-inch sticks, approx. ¼ inch thick)

2 cups celery sticks (2- to 3-inch sticks, approx. ¼ inch thick)

4 cups pickling vinegar (5% acidity)

¼ cup pickling salt

2 cups granulated sugar

2 tbsp mustard seeds

1 tbsp celery seeds

### INSTRUCTIONS

1   Fill your water canner roughly three-quarters full of water. Bring to a boil over high heat.

2   Prepare jars, bands, and lids for canning and keep warm (see page 33).

3   In a large bowl, prepare an ice bath. Bring a large pot of water to a boil. Working in batches, boil (blanch) each vegetable for 1 minute. Using a slotted spoon or spider, transfer blanched vegetables to the ice bath.

4   Make brine: In a large pot, combine vinegar, salt, sugar, mustard seeds, and celery seeds and bring to a boil. Heat, stirring occasionally, until the salt and sugar have completely dissolved.

5   Pack the vegetables tightly into prepared jars, leaving ½-inch headspace.

6   Ladle the hot brine over the vegetables, maintaining ½-inch headspace. Remove bubbles using a bubble remover (see page 34).

7   Using a clean, damp cloth or paper towel, wipe rims clean. Place sterilized lids on jars. Then screw on bands and tighten just until fingertip-tight (see page 34).

8   Using a jar lifter, place jars in canner rack. Submerge rack in boiling water, ensuring jars are covered by at least 1 inch of water. (You may need to add a little extra boiling water.) Cover canner with lid and bring water to a rolling boil.

9   Process jars for 10 minutes (adjust for altitude, if needed; see page 198). At end of processing time, turn off heat and remove lid.

10  Once water has stopped boiling, use jar lifter to carefully remove jars, without tilting, and place on a towel.

11  Let jars cool, undisturbed, for 12 to 24 hours. Once completely cool, test the seals by gently pressing down on the center of the lids—they should not flex (see page 35).

# MIXED GARDEN PICKLE

SUMMER/FALL | WATER BATH | YIELD: 6 (16-OZ) PINT JARS

*This vibrant medley of pickled vegetables is crisp, tangy, and packed with garden-fresh flavors. A delicious snack, side, or salad topper!*

## INGREDIENTS

2 cups chopped green beans (bite-size pieces)

2 cups cherry tomatoes

1 cup cauliflower florets

1 cup sliced carrots

4 cups pickling vinegar (5% acidity)

2 cups water

½ cup pickling salt

1 tbsp mixed pickling spices

## INSTRUCTIONS

1   Fill your water canner roughly three-quarters full of water. Bring to a boil over high heat.

2   Prepare jars, bands, and lids for canning and keep warm (see page 33).

3   In a large bowl, prepare an ice bath. Bring a large pot of water to a boil. Working in batches, boil (blanch) each vegetable for 1 minute. Using a slotted spoon or spider, transfer blanched vegetables to the ice bath.

4   Make brine: In a large pot, combine vinegar, water, salt, and pickling spices and bring to a boil. Heat, stirring occasionally, until the salt has completely dissolved.

5   Pack the vegetables tightly into jars, leaving ½-inch headspace.

6   Ladle the hot brine over the vegetables, maintaining ½-inch headspace. Remove bubbles using a bubble remover (see page 34).

7   Using a clean, damp cloth or paper towel, wipe rims clean. Place sterilized lids on jars. Then screw on bands and tighten just until fingertip-tight (see page 34).

8   Using a jar lifter, place jars in canner rack. Submerge rack in boiling water, ensuring jars are covered by at least 1 inch of water. (You may need to add a little extra boiling water.) Cover canner with lid and bring water to a rolling boil.

9   Process jars for 10 minutes (adjust for altitude, if needed; see page 198). At end of processing time, turn off heat and remove lid.

10  Once water has stopped boiling, use jar lifter to carefully remove jars, without tilting, and place on a towel.

11  Let jars cool, undisturbed, for 12 to 24 hours. Once completely cool, test the seals by gently pressing down on the center of the lids—they should not flex (see page 35).

# SWEET RELISH

## SUMMER/FALL | WATER BATH | YIELD: 6 (16-OZ) PINT JARS

*This classic sweet relish is the perfect balance of tangy and sweet. Ideal for burgers, hot dogs, or sandwiches, or as a zesty addition to potato or pasta salads.*

### INGREDIENTS

6 cups finely chopped cucumbers

2 cups finely chopped yellow or white onions

1 cup finely chopped green bell pepper

1 cup finely chopped red bell pepper

¼ cup pickling salt

3 cups pickling vinegar (5% acidity)

1½ cups granulated sugar

1 tbsp mustard seeds

1 tsp celery seeds

½ tsp ground turmeric

### INSTRUCTIONS

1  In a large bowl, combine chopped vegetables and salt. Set aside for 2 hours.

2  Transfer vegetables to a colander and rinse well under cool running water.

3  Fill your water canner roughly three-quarters full of water. Bring to a boil over high heat.

4  Prepare jars, bands, and lids for canning and keep warm (see page 33).

5  Make brine: In a large pot, combine vinegar, sugar, mustard seeds, celery seeds, and turmeric and bring to a boil. Heat, stirring occasionally, until the sugar has completely dissolved.

6  Add drained vegetables to the brine. Simmer for 10 minutes, stirring occasionally.

7  Ladle the hot relish into prepared jars, leaving ½-inch headspace. Remove bubbles using a bubble remover (see page 34).

8  Using a clean, damp cloth or paper towel, wipe rims clean. Place sterilized lids on jars. Then screw on bands and tighten just until fingertip-tight (see page 34).

9  Using a jar lifter, place jars in canner rack. Submerge rack in boiling water, ensuring jars are covered by at least 1 inch of water. (You may need to add a little extra boiling water.) Cover canner with lid and bring water to a rolling boil.

10  Process jars for 15 minutes (adjust for altitude, if needed; see page 198). At end of processing time, turn off heat and remove lid.

11  Once water has stopped boiling, use jar lifter to carefully remove jars, without tilting, and place on a towel.

12  Let jars cool, undisturbed, for 12 to 24 hours. Once completely cool, test the seals by gently pressing down on the center of the lids—they should not flex (see page 35).

# CORN RELISH

## SUMMER/FALL | WATER BATH | YIELD: 6 (16-OZ) PINT JARS

*Sweet and tangy, this corn relish is perfect for tacos or burgers, or as a side dish. It adds a bright, fresh flavor to any meal!*

### INGREDIENTS

5 cups pickling vinegar (5% acidity)

2 cups granulated sugar

2 tbsp mustard seeds

1 tbsp ground turmeric

1 tbsp celery seeds

10 cups fresh corn kernels (approx. 16 ears)

2 cups chopped sweet red peppers

1 cup chopped celery

### INSTRUCTIONS

1 Fill your water canner roughly three-quarters full of water. Bring to a boil over high heat.

2 Prepare jars, bands, and lids for canning and keep warm (see page 33).

3 Make brine: In a large pot, combine vinegar, sugar, mustard seeds, turmeric, and celery seeds and bring to a boil. Heat, stirring occasionally, until the sugar has completely dissolved.

4 Add corn, peppers, and celery to the brine. Simmer for 20 minutes.

5 Ladle the hot relish into prepared jars, leaving ½-inch headspace. Remove bubbles using a bubble remover (see page 34).

6 Using a clean, damp cloth or paper towel, wipe rims clean. Place sterilized lids on jars. Then screw on bands and tighten just until fingertip-tight (see page 34).

7 Using a jar lifter, place jars in canner rack. Submerge rack in boiling water, ensuring jars are covered by at least 1 inch of water. (You may need to add a little extra boiling water.) Cover canner with lid and bring water to a rolling boil.

8 Process jars for 15 minutes (adjust for altitude, if needed; see page 198). At end of processing time, turn off heat and remove lid.

9 Once water has stopped boiling, use jar lifter to carefully remove jars, without tilting, and place on a towel.

10 Let jars cool, undisturbed, for 12 to 24 hours. Once completely cool, test the seals by gently pressing down on the center of the lids—they should not flex (see page 35).

# POTATOES

YEAR-ROUND | PRESSURE CANNING | YIELD: 7 (32-OZ) QUART OR 9 (16-OZ) PINT JARS

*Whether you're making a hearty soup, a quick breakfast hash, or buttery mashed potatoes, having canned potatoes on hand means less prep time and more home-cooked meals with ease. Kids love them too. Pan-fry them with a little butter and a sprinkle of seasoning, and you've got a crispy, golden side dish in minutes.*

## INGREDIENTS

20 pounds white potatoes, cut into 1- to 2-inch cubes

7 tsp pickling salt, divided (1 tsp per quart, ½ tsp per pint; optional)

## INSTRUCTIONS

1. Prepare jars, bands, and lids for canning and keep warm (see page 49).

2. Prepare potatoes: Bring a large pot of water to a boil. Add potatoes to water and boil (blanch) for 10 minutes. Strain well.

3. To each jar, add salt (if using).

4. Pack the blanched potatoes loosely into prepared jars. Leave 1-inch headspace.

5. Pour boiling water over the potatoes, maintaining 1-inch headspace. Remove bubbles using a bubble remover (see page 49).

6. Using a clean, damp cloth or paper towel, wipe rims clean. Place sterilized lids on jars. Then screw on bands and tighten just until fingertip-tight (see page 49).

7. Fill your pressure canner with 2 to 3 inches of water. (Check your model's manual for exact recommendations.)

8. Load jars onto rack in pressure canner, ensuring they don't touch. Affix canner lid and turn heat to high.

9. Once canner is steaming, allow it to vent steam for 10 minutes before closing the vent or adding the weight (see page 50).

10. Bring canner to the correct PSI for your model and altitude (see page 199). Process pints for 25 minutes and quarts for 30 minutes. (Start timer only when canner reaches correct pressure.)

11. Turn off heat and allow the canner to cool naturally. Do not remove the lid or regulator until the pressure gauge reads zero. Tilt the lid away from your face when opening the canner.

12. Use jar lifter to carefully remove jars, without tilting, and place on a towel.

13. Let jars cool, undisturbed, for 12 to 24 hours. Once completely cool, test the seals by gently pressing down on the center of the lids—they should not flex (see page 52).

# CARROTS

**YEAR-ROUND | PRESSURE CANNING | YIELD: 7 (32-OZ) QUART OR 9 (16-OZ) PINT JARS**

*Carrots are one of the best vegetables for pressure canning. Not only do they retain their vibrant color and natural sweetness, but they also stay wonderfully firm, making them a pantry staple for quick meals. Whether you're tossing them into a hearty stew, glazing them with butter for a side dish, or simply enjoying them straight from the jar, home-canned carrots capture the best of their fresh-picked flavor.*

## INGREDIENTS

17 pounds fresh carrots, peeled and sliced or cubed, or leave whole

7 tsp pickling salt, divided (1 tsp per quart, ½ tsp per pint; optional)

Your choice of seasoning (see below)

**Optional Seasonings (per quart; halve quantities for pints)**

**Savory:** ½ tsp dried thyme or ½ tsp dried Italian seasoning

**Spiced:** ½ tsp ground cinnamon and ⅛ tsp ground nutmeg

**Dill and Peppercorn:** ½ tsp dried dill and 3 whole black peppercorns

**Curry:** ½ tsp curry powder

**Bay Leaf and Mustard Seed:** 1 small bay leaf plus ½ tsp mustard seeds

## INSTRUCTIONS

1   Prepare jars, bands, and lids for canning and keep warm (see page 49).

2   Prepare carrots: Blanching is optional but helps preserve color and texture. (For raw pack, skip blanching and pack raw carrots directly into jars.) In a large bowl, prepare an ice bath. Bring a large pot of water to a boil. Add carrots to water and boil (blanch) for 3 to 5 minutes (based on desired doneness). Using a slotted spoon or spider, transfer blanched carrots to the ice bath.

3   If using seasonings, divide equally among jars, along with salt.

4   Pack the carrots tightly into jars, but don't force them down. Leave 1-inch headspace.

5   Pour boiling water over carrots, maintaining 1-inch headspace. Remove bubbles using a bubble remover (see page 49).

6   Using a clean, damp cloth or paper towel, wipe rims clean. Place sterilized lids on jars. Then screw on bands and tighten just until fingertip-tight (see page 49).

7   Fill your pressure canner with 2 to 3 inches of water. (Check your model's manual for exact recommendations.)

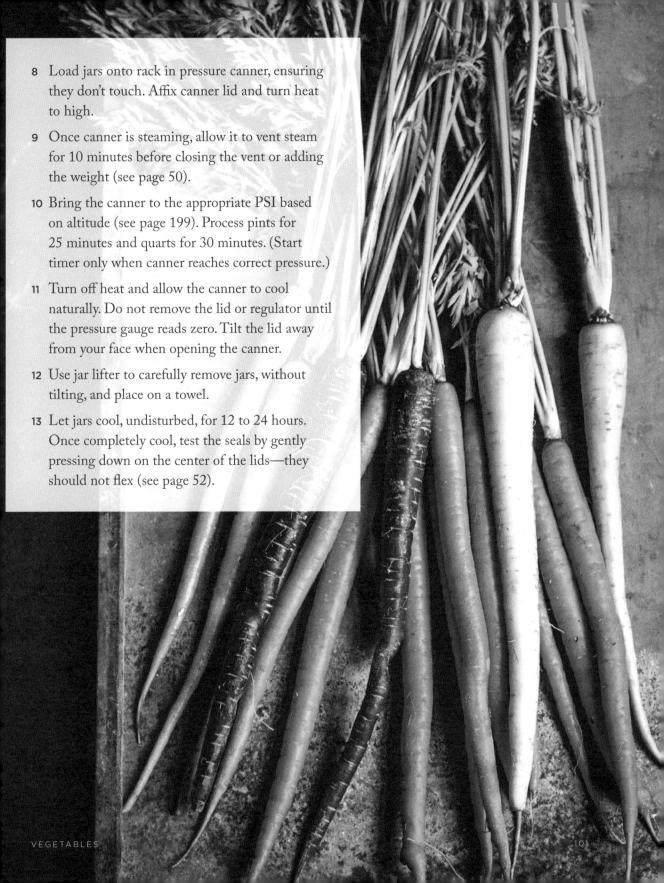

8  Load jars onto rack in pressure canner, ensuring they don't touch. Affix canner lid and turn heat to high.

9  Once canner is steaming, allow it to vent steam for 10 minutes before closing the vent or adding the weight (see page 50).

10  Bring the canner to the appropriate PSI based on altitude (see page 199). Process pints for 25 minutes and quarts for 30 minutes. (Start timer only when canner reaches correct pressure.)

11  Turn off heat and allow the canner to cool naturally. Do not remove the lid or regulator until the pressure gauge reads zero. Tilt the lid away from your face when opening the canner.

12  Use jar lifter to carefully remove jars, without tilting, and place on a towel.

13  Let jars cool, undisturbed, for 12 to 24 hours. Once completely cool, test the seals by gently pressing down on the center of the lids—they should not flex (see page 52).

# MIXED VEGETABLES

**YEAR-ROUND | PRESSURE CANNING | YIELD: 7 (32-OZ) QUART OR 9 (16-OZ) PINT JARS**

*The key to preserving the bright colors and fresh texture of this mixed vegetable medley lies in a few simple tricks. Blanching the vegetables before canning helps maintain their vibrant hues and prevents them from becoming overly soft during processing. Using high-quality, fresh-picked produce ensures peak flavor and texture—older vegetables may lose their firmness. To keep flavors balanced, opt for a light salt brine or broth instead of plain water, which enhances taste without overpowering. Lastly, cooling jars slowly and storing them in a dark, cool pantry will prevent color fading over time.*

### INGREDIENTS

4 pounds carrots, peeled and diced

3 pounds green beans, trimmed and cut into 1-inch pieces

2 pounds peas, shelled

1 pound fresh corn kernels (approx. 5 ears)

7 tsp pickling salt, divided (1 tsp per quart, ½ tsp per pint; optional)

### INSTRUCTIONS

1   Prepare jars, bands, and lids for canning and keep warm (see page 49).

2   Prepare vegetables in separate batches: In a large bowl, prepare an ice bath. Bring a large pot of water to a boil. Add vegetables to the water and boil (blanch) for 2 to 3 minutes. Using a slotted spoon or spider, transfer blanched vegetables to the ice bath. Once cooled, transfer vegetables to a large bowl and gently mix to distribute the vegetables evenly.

3   Divide the salt evenly among jars (if using).

4   Pack the blanched mixed vegetables loosely into jars, leaving 1-inch headspace.

5   Pour boiling water over vegetables, maintaining 1-inch headspace. Remove bubbles using a bubble remover (see page 49).

6   Using a clean, damp cloth or paper towel, wipe rims clean. Place sterilized lids on jars. Then screw on bands and tighten just until fingertip-tight (see page 49).

7   Fill your pressure canner with 2 to 3 inches of water. (Check your model's manual for exact recommendations.)

8   Load jars onto rack in pressure canner, ensuring they don't touch. Affix canner lid and turn heat to high.

9   Once canner is steaming, allow it to vent steam for 10 minutes before closing the vent or adding the weight (see page 50).

10  Bring canner to the correct PSI for your model
and altitude (see page 199). Process pints for
75 minutes and quarts for 90 minutes. (Start
timer only when canner reaches correct pressure.)

11  Turn off heat and allow the canner to cool
naturally. Do not remove the lid or regulator until
the pressure gauge reads zero. Tilt the lid away
from your face when opening the canner.

12  Use jar lifter to carefully remove jars, without
tilting, and place on a towel.

13  Let jars cool, undisturbed, for 12 to 24 hours.
Once completely cool, test the seals by gently
pressing down on the center of the lids—they
should not flex (see page 52).

# PUMPKIN

FALL | PRESSURE CANNING | YIELD: 7 (32-OZ) QUART OR 9 (16-OZ) PINT JARS

*As a pumpkin-pie lover, I can say with confidence that canning cubed pumpkin is the best way to make pies completely from scratch. Just pop open a jar, drain the liquid, and mash the softened pumpkin—it blends into the smoothest, freshest purée, with no need for canned store-bought varieties. (See page 43 for guidance on canning pumpkin and other squash.)*

## INGREDIENTS

16 pounds fresh pie pumpkins, seeded, peeled, and cubed (do not purée)

7 tsp pickling salt, divided (1 tsp per quart, ½ tsp per pint; optional)

## INSTRUCTIONS

1  Prepare jars, bands, and lids for canning and keep warm (see page 49).

2  Prepare pumpkin: Bring a large pot of water to a boil. Add pumpkin and boil (blanch) for 2 minutes. Strain well.

3  Divide salt evenly among jars (if using).

4  Pack the blanched pumpkin loosely into jars. Leave 1-inch headspace.

5  Pour boiling water over pumpkin, maintaining 1-inch headspace. Remove bubbles using a bubble remover (see page 49).

6  Using a clean, damp cloth or paper towel, wipe rims clean. Place sterilized lids on jars. Then screw on bands and tighten just until fingertip-tight (see page 49).

7  Fill your pressure canner with 2 to 3 inches of water. (Check your model's manual for exact recommendations.)

8  Load jars onto rack in pressure canner, ensuring they don't touch. Affix canner lid and turn heat to high.

9  Once canner is steaming, allow it to vent steam for 10 minutes before closing the vent or adding the weight (see page 50).

10  Bring canner to the correct PSI for your model and altitude (see page 199). Process pints for 55 minutes and quarts for 90 minutes. (Start timer only when canner reaches correct pressure.)

11  Turn off heat and allow the canner to cool naturally. Do not remove the lid or regulator until the pressure gauge reads zero. Tilt the lid away from your face when opening the canner.

12  Use jar lifter to carefully remove jars, without tilting, and place on a towel.

13 Let jars cool, undisturbed, for 12 to 24 hours. Once completely cool, test the seals by gently pressing down on the center of the lids—they should not flex (see page 52).

# CORN

*To prepare corn for canning, husk the ears and remove all silk, using a vegetable brush or damp paper towel for stubborn strands. Cut the kernels off the cob with a sharp knife or corn stripper, staying close to the cob but avoiding the tough, starchy base. For creamed corn, skip the dairy. Preserve whole-kernel corn instead, and blend or simmer it with butter and milk when ready to serve (see recipe on page 107).*

### INGREDIENTS

31 pounds fresh whole-kernel sweet corn, niblets cut from cobs (see Tip)

7 tsp pickling salt, divided (1 tsp per quart, ½ tsp per pint; optional)

### INSTRUCTIONS

1 Prepare jars, bands, and lids for canning and keep warm (see page 49).

2 Prepare corn kernels: Bring a large pot of water to a boil. Add corn and boil (blanch) for 3 minutes. Strain well.

3 Divide the salt evenly among jars (if using).

4 Pack the blanched corn loosely into jars. Leave 1-inch headspace.

5 Pour boiling water over the corn, maintaining 1-inch headspace. Remove bubbles using a bubble remover (see page 49).

6 Using a clean, damp cloth or paper towel, wipe rims clean. Place sterilized lids on jars. Then screw on bands and tighten just until fingertip-tight (see page 49).

7 Fill your pressure canner with 2 to 3 inches of water. (Check your model's manual for exact recommendations.)

8 Load jars onto rack in pressure canner, ensuring they don't touch. Affix canner lid and turn heat to high.

9 Once canner is steaming, allow it to vent steam for 10 minutes before closing the vent or adding the weight (see page 50).

10 Bring canner to the correct PSI for your model and altitude (see page 199). Process pints for 55 minutes and quarts for 85 minutes. (Start timer only when canner reaches correct pressure.)

11 Turn off heat and allow the canner to cool naturally. Do not remove the lid or regulator until the pressure gauge reads zero. Tilt the lid away from your face when opening the canner.

12 Use jar lifter to carefully remove jars, without tilting, and place on a towel.

**13** Let jars cool, undisturbed, for 12 to 24 hours. Once completely cool, test the seals by gently pressing down on the center of the lids—they should not flex (see page 52).

TIP

To keep kernels from scattering when cutting, stand the corn upright in the center of a Bundt pan or inside a large, shallow bowl. The pan's hole or bowl edges will stabilize the cob while catching the kernels as you slice downward with a sharp knife. This method keeps your workspace neat and makes cleanup a breeze!

## BASIC CREAMED CORN

To make creamed corn, melt 2 tbsp butter in a large saucepan. Whisk in ½ cup heavy cream or whole milk, 1 tbsp cornstarch mixed with 2 tbsp cold water (for a smooth texture), ½ tsp salt (or to taste), ¼ tsp black pepper, and 1 tsp granulated sugar (optional, enhances sweetness). Add 1 pint (2¼ cups) drained home-canned corn plus ½ cup canning liquid. Bring to a boil over medium heat, reduce heat and simmer, stirring frequently, for 1 to 2 minutes, until thickened to your preferred consistency. (For a quart of canned corn, double the quantity of ingredients.)

# SWEET POTATOES

**FALL/WINTER | PRESSURE CANNING | YIELD: 7 (32-OZ) QUART OR 9 (16-OZ) PINT JARS**

*Parboiling sweet potatoes before canning is key! It helps sweet potatoes hold their shape during pressure canning. Once opened, refrigerate any leftovers and use them within a week—though in my house, they never last that long! Whether I'm whipping up a holiday favorite or a weeknight side, I love knowing that a jar of sweet potatoes is always within reach.*

### INGREDIENTS

16 pounds medium sweet potatoes, peeled and cut into 1-inch cubes

7 tsp pickling salt, divided (1 tsp per quart or ½ tsp per pint; optional)

### INSTRUCTIONS

1 Prepare jars, bands, and lids for canning and keep warm (see page 49).

2 Prepare sweet potatoes: Bring a large pot of water to a boil. Add sweet potatoes and boil (blanch) for 2 minutes. Strain well.

3 Divide salt evenly among prepared jars (if using).

4 Pack sweet potatoes loosely into jars. Leave 1-inch headspace.

5 Pour boiling water over sweet potatoes, maintaining 1-inch headspace. Remove bubbles using a bubble remover (see page 49).

6 Using a clean, damp cloth or paper towel, wipe rims clean. Place sterilized lids on jars. Then screw on bands and tighten just until fingertip-tight (see page 49).

7 Fill your pressure canner with 2 to 3 inches of water. (Check your model's manual for exact recommendations.)

8 Load jars onto rack in pressure canner, ensuring they don't touch. Affix canner lid and turn heat to high.

9 Once canner is steaming, allow it to vent steam for 10 minutes before closing the vent or adding the weight (see page 50).

10 Bring canner to the correct PSI for your model and altitude (see page 199). Process pints for 65 minutes and quarts for 95 minutes. (Start timer only when canner reaches correct pressure.)

11 Turn off heat and allow the canner to cool naturally. Do not remove the lid or regulator until the pressure gauge reads zero. Tilt the lid away from your face when opening the canner.

12 Use jar lifter to carefully remove jars, without tilting, and place on a towel.

13 Let jars cool, undisturbed, for 12 to 24 hours. Once completely cool, test the seals by gently pressing down on the center of the lids—they should not flex (see page 52).

# WINTER SQUASH

**FALL/WINTER | PRESSURE CANNING | YIELD: 7 (32-OZ) QUART OR 9 (16-OZ) PINT JARS**

*Winter squash is a versatile, nutrient-packed ingredient that's ready at a moment's notice. For a cozy meal, blend it into a creamy soup or toss the tender cubes into a hearty stew. For a quick and flavorful side dish, mash the squash and mix it with butter, maple syrup, or warming spices.*

### INGREDIENTS

16 pounds winter squash (e.g., butternut, acorn, or other varieties), seeded, peeled, and cut into 1-inch cubes

7 tsp pickling salt, divided (1 tsp per quart, ½ tsp per pint; optional)

### INSTRUCTIONS

1   Prepare jars, bands, and lids for canning and keep warm (see page 49).

2   Prepare squash: Bring a large pot of water to a boil. Add squash and boil (blanch) for 2 minutes. Strain well.

3   Divide salt evenly among jars (if using).

4   Pack squash loosely into prepared jars. Leave 1-inch headspace.

5   Pour boiling water over the squash, maintaining 1-inch headspace. Remove bubbles using a bubble remover (see page 49).

6   Using a clean, damp cloth or paper towel, wipe rims clean. Place sterilized lids on jars. Then screw on bands and tighten just until fingertip-tight (see page 49).

7   Fill your pressure canner with 2 to 3 inches of water. (Check your model's manual for exact recommendations.)

8   Load jars onto rack in pressure canner, ensuring they don't touch. Affix canner lid and turn heat to high.

9   Once canner is steaming, allow it to vent steam for 10 minutes before closing the vent or adding the weight (see page 50).

10  Bring canner to the correct PSI for your model and altitude (see page 199). Process pints for 55 minutes and quarts for 90 minutes. (Start timer only when canner reaches correct pressure.)

11  Turn off heat and allow the canner to cool naturally. Do not remove the lid or regulator until the pressure gauge reads zero. Tilt the lid away from your face when opening the canner.

12  Use jar lifter to carefully remove jars, without tilting, and place on a towel.

13  Let jars cool, undisturbed, for 12 to 24 hours. Once completely cool, test the seals by gently pressing down on the center of the lids—they should not flex (see page 52).

# MIXED BRAISING GREENS

**SPRING/SUMER | PRESSURE CANNING | YIELD: 7 (32-OZ) QUART OR 9 (16-OZ) PINT JARS**

*Leafy greens like spinach, kale, and chard are packed with nutrients, and pressure canning is a great way to preserve their goodness for easy use in soups, stews, and sautés. However, blanching is a crucial step before canning. Blanching wilts the greens, allowing you to pack more into each jar while also removing air pockets that cause uneven heating during pressure canning. It also preserves color, texture, and nutrients by stopping enzymatic activity that lead to loss of flavor and quality over time. Without blanching, greens become overly tough or mushy after canning, making them less enjoyable in recipes. Once canned, these greens are incredibly versatile. Drain and sauté with garlic, fold in smoked ham, or add a splash of vinegar for a brighter flavor profile.*

### INGREDIENTS

28 pounds fresh greens (e.g., spinach, kale, chard, or other varieties), tough stems trimmed and discarded

7 tsp pickling salt, divided (1 tsp per quart, ½ tsp per pint; optional)

### INSTRUCTIONS

1　Prepare jars, bands, and lids for canning and keep warm (see page 49).

2　Prepare greens: In a large bowl, prepare an ice bath. Bring a large pot of water to a boil. Add greens to water and boil (blanch) for 2 minutes.

3　Using a slotted spoon or spider, transfer blanched greens to the ice bath. Once cooled, transfer greens to a large bowl and gently mix to distribute the vegetables evenly.

4　Divide salt evenly among jars (if using).

5　Pack greens loosely into jars. Leave 1-inch headspace.

6　Pour boiling water over potatoes, maintaining 1-inch headspace. Remove bubbles using a bubble remover (see page 49).

7　Using a clean, damp cloth or paper towel, wipe rims clean. Place sterilized lids on jars. Then screw on bands and tighten just until fingertip-tight (see page 49).

8　Fill your pressure canner with 2 to 3 inches of water. (Check your model's manual for exact recommendations.)

9　Load jars onto rack in pressure canner, ensuring they don't touch. Affix canner lid and turn heat to high.

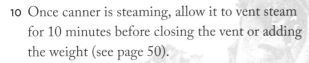

10  Once canner is steaming, allow it to vent steam for 10 minutes before closing the vent or adding the weight (see page 50).

11  Bring canner to the correct PSI for your model and altitude (see page 199). Process pints for 70 minutes and quarts for 90 minutes. (Start timer only when canner reaches correct pressure.)

12  Turn off heat and allow the canner to cool naturally. Do not remove the lid or regulator until the pressure gauge reads zero. Tilt the lid away from your face when opening the canner.

13  Use jar lifter to carefully remove jars, without tilting, and place on a towel.

14  Let jars cool, undisturbed, for 12 to 24 hours. Once completely cool, test the seals by gently pressing down on the center of the lids—they should not flex (see page 52).

# MUSHROOMS

**YEAR-ROUND | PRESSURE CANNING | YIELD: 9 (16-OZ) PINT OR 18 (8-OZ) HALF-PINT JARS**

*Home canning is an incredible way to save money on bulk mushrooms. Look for deals at farmers markets, restaurant supply stores, food co-ops, or local farms that sell fresh mushrooms in large quantities. Canned mushrooms bring instant depth and richness to dishes, from creamy risottos to slow-cooked stews. Just avoid canning in quarts for mushrooms—they don't hold up well.*

### INGREDIENTS

14 pounds button mushrooms, trimmed (see Tip)

7 tsp pickling salt, divided (½ tsp per pint or ¼ tsp per half-pint, optional)

### INSTRUCTIONS

1   Prepare jars, bands, and lids for canning and keep warm (see page 49).

2   Prepare mushrooms: Bring a large pot of water to a boil. Add mushrooms and boil (blanch) for 5 minutes. Strain well.

3   Divide salt evenly among jars (if using).

4   Pack mushrooms loosely into jars. Leave 1-inch headspace.

5   Pour boiling water over mushrooms, maintaining 1-inch headspace. Remove bubbles using a bubble remover (see page 49).

6   Using a clean, damp cloth or paper towel, wipe rims clean. Place sterilized lids on jars. Then screw on bands and tighten just until fingertip-tight (see page 49).

7   Fill your pressure canner with 2 to 3 inches of water. (Check your model's manual for exact recommendations.)

8   Load jars onto rack in pressure canner, ensuring they don't touch. Affix canner lid and turn heat to high.

9   Once canner is steaming, allow it to vent steam for 10 minutes before closing the vent or adding the weight (see page 50).

10  Bring canner to the correct PSI for your model and altitude (see page 199). Process both half-pints and full pints for 45 minutes. (Start timer only when canner reaches correct pressure.)

11  Turn off heat and allow the canner to cool naturally. Do not remove the lid or regulator until the pressure gauge reads zero. Tilt the lid away from your face when opening the canner.

12  Use jar lifter to carefully remove jars, without tilting, and place on a towel.

**13** Let jars cool, undisturbed, for 12 to 24 hours. Once completely cool, test the seals by gently pressing down on the center of the lids—they should not flex (see page 52).

---

### TIP

Mushrooms absorb water easily, so avoid soaking them when cleaning. Instead, gently wipe each mushroom with a damp paper towel, soft brush, or clean cloth to remove dirt. If needed, give them a quick rinse under cold running water and pat dry immediately. Trim off any tough stems, and for even cooking and canning, halve or quarter larger mushrooms so they're uniform in size. Keeping the pieces similar ensures they process evenly and absorb liquid at the same rate, giving you the best texture in every jar.

CHAPTER 7

# SAUCES AND CHUTNEYS

**WATER BATH CANNING**

| | |
|---|---|
| Marinara Sauce | 116 |
| Pizza Sauce | 118 |
| Ketchup | 120 |
| BBQ Sauce | 122 |
| Tomato Chutney | 124 |
| Apple Chutney | 126 |
| Peach Salsa | 128 |

**PRESSURE CANNING**

| | |
|---|---|
| Garden Vegetable Sauce | 130 |
| Mixed Pepper Sauce | 132 |
| Mushroom Sauce | 134 |
| Meat Sauce | 136 |

# SAUCE CONSISTENCY GUIDE

Achieving the perfect texture for your sauces is as much about preparation as it is about technique. Here's a quick guide to help you make beautifully thick and balanced sauces every time.

## PROPER THICKENING

**Tomato-based sauces:** Simmer your sauce, uncovered, over medium heat to allow water to evaporate naturally. Stir frequently to prevent sticking.

**Vegetable-based sauces:** Purée vegetables like carrots, zucchini, or mushrooms to naturally thicken sauces without added thickeners.

**Thick sauces (e.g., BBQ, ketchup):** Add a small amount of tomato paste for extra body. Use a potato masher or immersion blender for smoother consistency.

## ADJUSTING THICKNESS

**If your sauce is too thick:** Stir in small amounts of broth, tomato juice, or water, and then simmer to meld flavors.

**If your sauce is too thin:** Continue simmering to reduce the liquid or add tomato paste or puréed vegetables.

## TESTING METHODS

Allow sauce to cool briefly before testing, as hot liquids may appear thinner. Then use a spoon to check the sauce's texture:

For pourable sauces (e.g., marinara), the sauce should coat the back of the spoon lightly.

For thicker sauces (e.g., ketchup), the sauce should mound slightly on the spoon.

After processing, sauces may thicken slightly as they cool. Keep this in mind and ensure proper headspace to allow for safe heat distribution. Always stir the sauce well before serving.

# MARINARA SAUCE

**SUMMER/FALL | WATER BATH | YIELD: 6 (16-OZ) PINT JARS**

*This classic Italian marinara sauce is a pantry staple, perfect for pasta, lasagna, or pizza. Made with fresh tomatoes, basil, and oregano, it's rich, versatile, and easy to customize with spice or depth.*

## INGREDIENTS

10 pounds ripe tomatoes (approx. 30 medium tomatoes)

¼ cup olive oil

1 large yellow onion, diced

4 cloves garlic, minced

½ cup chopped fresh basil leaves or 2 tbsp dried basil

2 tsp dried oregano

1 tbsp sea salt (optional)

12 tsp citric acid or 12 tbsp bottled lemon juice, divided

## INSTRUCTIONS

1  Prepare tomatoes: In a large bowl, prepare an ice bath. Bring a large pot of water to a boil. Meanwhile, using a paring knife, cut a small X on the bottom of each tomato. Add tomatoes to water and boil (blanch) for 30 to 60 seconds. Using a slotted spoon or spider, transfer blanched tomatoes to the ice bath. Peel the skins and cut away any blemished areas. Core the tomatoes. Dice for a chunky sauce, or crush for a smoother consistency.

2  In a large stockpot over medium heat, heat the oil. Add onion and garlic, and sauté until fragrant, about 3 minutes. Stir in prepared tomatoes, basil, oregano, and salt (if using). Stir to combine. Reduce heat and simmer, stirring occasionally, until the sauce thickens to your preference, 1 to 2 hours.

3  Fill your water canner roughly three-quarters full of water. Bring to a boil over high heat.

4  Prepare jars, bands, and lids for canning and keep warm (see page 33).

5  To each prepared jar, add 2 tsp citric acid or 2 tbsp lemon juice.

6  Ladle the hot marina sauce into jars, leaving ½-inch headspace. Remove bubbles using a bubble remover (see page 34).

7  Using a clean, damp cloth or paper towel, wipe rims clean. Place sterilized lids on jars. Then screw on bands and tighten just until fingertip-tight (see page 34).

8  Using a jar lifter, place jars in canner rack. Submerge rack in boiling water, ensuring jars are covered by at least 1 inch of water. (You may need to add a little extra boiling water.) Cover canner with lid and bring water to a rolling boil.

9 Process jars for 35 minutes (adjust for altitude, if needed; see page 198). At end of processing time, turn off heat and remove lid.

10 Once water has stopped boiling, use jar lifter to carefully remove jars, without tilting, and place on a towel.

11 Let jars cool, undisturbed, for 12 to 24 hours. Once completely cool, test the seals by gently pressing down on the center of the lids—they should not flex (see page 35).

---

### VARIATIONS

In Step 2, stir in ¼ tsp crushed red pepper flakes to add a little heat.

In Step 2, stir in ¼ cup dry red wine for added richness.

# PIZZA SAUCE

SUMMER | WATER BATH | YIELD: 6 (16-OZ) PINT JARS

*This rich and herby pizza sauce is perfectly seasoned for homemade pizzas and can also double as a flavorful pasta base. Customize with extra spice or bold herbal notes to match your taste.*

## INGREDIENTS

10 pounds ripe tomatoes, peeled, cored, and crushed

¼ cup olive oil

1 medium onion, diced

4 cloves garlic, minced

2 tbsp dried oregano

1 tbsp dried basil

½ tsp freshly ground black pepper

½ tsp sea salt (optional)

12 tsp citric acid or 12 tbsp bottled lemon juice, divided

## INSTRUCTIONS

1   Prepare tomatoes: In a large bowl, prepare an ice bath. Bring a large pot of water to a boil. Meanwhile, using a paring knife, cut a small X on the bottom of each tomato. Add tomatoes to water and boil (blanch) for 30 to 60 seconds. Using a slotted spoon or spider, transfer blanched tomatoes to the ice bath. Peel the skins and cut away any blemished areas. Core the tomatoes. Process in a blender or food processor for a smooth sauce or hand-crush for a chunkier texture.

2   In a large stockpot over medium heat, heat the oil. Add onions and garlic, and sauté until fragrant, about 3 minutes. Stir in prepared tomatoes, oregano, basil, pepper, and salt (if using). Stir to combine. Reduce heat and simmer, stirring occasionally, until the sauce thickens to your preference, 1 to 2 hours.

3   Fill your water canner roughly three-quarters full of water. Bring to a boil over high heat.

4   Prepare jars, bands, and lids for canning and keep warm (see page 33).

5   To each prepared jar, add 2 tsp citric acid or 2 tbsp lemon juice.

6   Ladle the hot pizza sauce into jars, leaving ½-inch headspace. Remove bubbles using a bubble remover (see page 34).

7   Using a clean, damp cloth or paper towel, wipe rims clean. Place sterilized lids on jars. Then screw on bands and tighten just until fingertip-tight (see page 34).

8   Using a jar lifter, place jars in canner rack. Submerge rack in boiling water, ensuring jars are covered by at least 1 inch of water. (You may need to add a little extra boiling water.) Cover canner with lid and bring water to a rolling boil.

9   Process jars for 35 minutes (adjust for altitude, if needed; see page 198). At end of processing time, turn off heat and remove lid.

10  Once water has stopped boiling, use jar lifter to carefully remove jars, without tilting, and place on a towel.

11  Let jars cool, undisturbed, for 12 to 24 hours. Once completely cool, test the seals by gently pressing down on the center of the lids—they should not flex (see page 35).

---

### VARIATIONS

In Step 1, stir in ¼ tsp crushed red pepper flakes to add a little heat.

After opening jar and before use, stir in ¼ cup finely grated Parmesan cheese.

# KETCHUP

**YEAR-ROUND | WATER BATH | YIELD: 4 (16-OZ) PINT JARS**

*There's something deeply satisfying about making your own ketchup—a kitchen staple that's usually over-looked when it comes to homemade alternatives. This version is nothing like the overly sweet, one-note store-bought kind. It's rich, tangy, and layered with spices that bring out the best in every bite. Canning a batch means you'll always have a jar on hand, ready for burgers, roasted potatoes, or as a secret ingredient in sauces and marinades.*

## INGREDIENTS

10 pounds ripe tomatoes, peeled, cored, and chopped

1½ cups apple cider vinegar (5% acidity)

1 cup packed brown sugar

½ cup granulated sugar

1 medium yellow onion, finely diced

3 cloves garlic, minced

1 tbsp sea salt

1 tsp ground cinnamon

½ tsp ground cloves

½ tsp ground allspice

½ tsp mustard powder

½ tsp freshly ground black pepper

¼ tsp cayenne pepper (optional)

2 tbsp tomato paste

## INSTRUCTIONS

1   In a large stockpot, combine chopped tomatoes, vinegar, brown sugar, granulated sugar, onion, garlic, salt, cinnamon, cloves, allspice, mustard powder, black pepper, and cayenne (if using). Bring the mixture to a gentle boil over medium-high heat, then reduce heat and simmer for 1½ to 2 hours, stirring occasionally until the tomatoes break down and the mixture thickens.

2   Using an immersion blender, blend the mixture until smooth. Alternatively, working in batches, transfer mixture to a blender and blend until smooth, then return it to the pot.

3   Stir in tomato paste and simmer, stirring frequently, for 30 to 45 minutes, until the ketchup reaches your desired thickness.

4   Meanwhile, prepare jars, bands, and lids for canning and keep warm (see page 33).

5   Ladle the hot ketchup into prepared jars, leaving ½-inch headspace. Remove bubbles using a bubble remover (see page 34).

6   Using a clean, damp cloth or paper towel, wipe rims clean to ensure a proper seal. Place sterilized lids on jars. Then screw on bands and tighten just until fingertip-tight (see page 34).

7   Fill your water canner roughly three-quarters full of water. Bring to a boil over high heat.

8   Using a jar lifter, place jars in canner rack. Submerge rack in boiling water, ensuring jars are covered by at least 1 inch of water. (You may need to add a little extra boiling water.) Cover canner with lid and bring water to a rolling boil.

9   Process jars for 15 minutes (adjust for altitude, if needed; see page 198). At end of processing time, turn off heat and remove lid.

10  Once water has stopped boiling, use jar lifter to carefully remove jars, without tilting, and place on a towel.

11  Let jars cool, undisturbed, for 12 to 24 hours. Once completely cool, test the seals by gently pressing down on the center of the lids—they should not flex (see page 35).

---

## VARIATIONS

**Garlic-Infused Ketchup:** In Step 1, stir in ¼ tsp garlic powder.

**Gourmet Balsamic Ketchup:** Substitute balsamic vinegar (5% acidity) for the apple cider vinegar.

**Smoky Ketchup:** In Step 1, stir in ¼ tsp smoked paprika.

# BBQ SAUCE

YEAR-ROUND | WATER BATH | YIELD: 4 (16-OZ) PINT JARS

*This smoky, tangy, and slightly sweet BBQ sauce is a must-have condiment for grilling, dipping (for fries, wings, or roasted veggies), and marinating. Stir it into baked beans for a bold, tangy twist, or serve it as a sauce for a jerk-marinated pork loin.*

## INGREDIENTS

10 pounds ripe tomatoes, peeled, cored, and chopped

1½ cups apple cider vinegar (5% acidity)

¾ cup molasses

¾ cup packed brown sugar

½ cup liquid honey or pure maple syrup (optional)

1 medium yellow onion, finely diced

3 cloves garlic, minced

2 tbsp Worcestershire sauce

1 tbsp smoked paprika

1 tbsp mustard powder

1 tsp ground cumin

1 tsp freshly ground black pepper

½ tsp ground cinnamon

½ tsp chili powder

½ tsp sea salt

¼ tsp ground cloves

2 tbsp tomato paste

## INSTRUCTIONS

1   In a large stockpot, combine chopped tomatoes, vinegar, molasses, brown sugar, honey (if using), onion, garlic, Worcestershire sauce, paprika, mustard powder, cumin, black pepper, cinnamon, chili powder, salt, and cloves. Bring the mixture to a gentle boil over medium-high heat, then reduce heat and simmer for 1½ to 2 hours, stirring occasionally, until the tomatoes break down and the mixture thickens.

2   Using an immersion blender, purée the mixture until smooth. Alternatively, working in batches, transfer mixture to a blender and blend until smooth, then return it to the pot.

3   Stir in tomato paste and simmer, stirring frequently, for 30 to 45 minutes, until the sauce reaches your desired thickness.

4   Meanwhile, prepare jars, bands, and lids for canning and keep warm (see page 33).

5   Ladle the hot BBQ sauce into prepared jars, leaving ½-inch headspace. Remove bubbles using a bubble remover (see page 34).

6   Using a clean, damp cloth or paper towel, wipe rims clean to ensure a proper seal. Place sterilized lids on jars. Then screw on bands and tighten just until fingertip-tight (see page 34).

7   Fill your water canner roughly three-quarters full of water. Bring to a boil over high heat.

8   Using a jar lifter, place jars in canner rack. Submerge rack in boiling water, ensuring jars are covered by at least 1 inch of water. (You may need to add a little extra boiling water.) Cover canner with lid and bring water to a rolling boil.

9   Process jars for 25 minutes (adjust for altitude, if needed; see page 198). At end of processing time, turn off heat and remove lid.

10  Once water has stopped boiling, use jar lifter to carefully remove jars, without tilting, and place on a towel.

11  Let jars cool, undisturbed, for 12 to 24 hours. Once completely cool, test the seals by gently pressing down on the center of the lids—they should not flex (see page 35).

---

## VARIATIONS

**Spicy BBQ Sauce:** In Step 1, add ½ tsp cayenne pepper.

**Smoky Hickory BBQ Sauce:** At the end of Step 5, stir in 1 tsp liquid smoke, then proceed with jarring.

**Sweet and Tangy BBQ Sauce:** Substitute balsamic vinegar (5% acidity) for the apple cider vinegar.

# TOMATO CHUTNEY

**LATE SUMMER/FALL | WATER BATH | YIELD: 5 (16-OZ) PINT JARS**

*There's nothing quite like a spoonful of this sweet and tangy tomato chutney to elevate any dish. Pair it with grilled meats, spoon it over roasted vegetables, or serve it alongside aged cheeses—it's sure to please.*

## INGREDIENTS

6 pounds ripe tomatoes, peeled, cored, and chopped

2 cups apple cider vinegar (5% acidity)

1½ cups packed brown sugar

½ cup granulated sugar

1 medium yellow onion, finely diced

2 cloves garlic, minced

1 tbsp grated fresh ginger

1 tbsp Worcestershire sauce

1 tsp mustard seeds

1 tsp ground cumin

1 tsp ground coriander

1 tsp smoked paprika

½ tsp ground cinnamon

½ tsp ground cloves

½ tsp chili powder (optional)

½ tsp sea salt

½ tsp freshly ground black pepper

½ cup golden raisins

## INSTRUCTIONS

1   In a large stockpot, combine chopped tomatoes, vinegar, brown sugar, granulated sugar, onion, garlic, ginger, Worcestershire sauce, mustard seeds, cumin, coriander, paprika, cinnamon, cloves, chili powder (if using), salt, pepper, and golden raisins. Bring the mixture to a gentle boil over medium-high heat, then reduce heat and simmer for 1½ to 2 hours, stirring occasionally until the tomatoes break down and the mixture thickens.

2   Using an immersion blender, purée the mixture until smooth. Alternatively, working in batches, transfer mixture to a blender and blend until smooth, then return it to the pot.

3   Simmer chutney, stirring frequently, for 30 to 45 minutes, until it reaches your desired thickness.

4   Meanwhile, prepare jars, bands, and lids for canning and keep warm (see page 33).

5   Ladle the hot chutney into prepared jars, leaving ½-inch headspace. Remove bubbles using a bubble remover (see page 34).

6   Using a clean, damp cloth or paper towel, wipe rims clean. Place sterilized lids on jars. Then screw on bands and tighten just until fingertip-tight (see page 34).

7   Fill your water canner roughly three-quarters full of water. Bring to a boil over high heat.

8   Using a jar lifter, place jars in canner rack. Submerge rack in boiling water, ensuring jars are covered by at least 1 inch of water. (You may need to add a little extra boiling water.) Cover canner with lid and bring water to a rolling boil.

9   Process jars for 30 minutes (adjust for altitude, if needed; see page 198). At end of processing time, turn off heat and remove lid.

10  Once water has stopped boiling, use jar lifter to carefully remove jars, without tilting, and place on a towel.

11  Let jars cool, undisturbed, for 12 to 24 hours. Once completely cool, test the seals by gently pressing down on the center of the lids—they should not flex (see page 35).

## VARIATIONS

**Fruity Chutney:** In Step 1, incorporate ½ cup chopped dried apricots or unsweetened dried cranberries along with the golden raisins.

**Herbed Chutney:** In Step 1, stir in 2 tbsp of chopped fresh cilantro or mint during the last 5 minutes of cooking.

**Spicy Tomato Chutney:** In Step 1, add ½ tsp cayenne pepper.

# APPLE CHUTNEY

## FALL | WATER BATH | YIELD: 4 (16-OZ) PINT JARS

*This sweet and tangy chutney is a perfect accompaniment to cheese boards, roasted meats, or sandwiches. Pair with sharp cheddar cheese or serve alongside roasted meats for a flavorful contrast. Use as a sandwich spread or stir into grain bowls for a tangy kick.*

### INGREDIENTS

4 pounds tart apples, peeled, cored, and chopped

1½ cups apple cider vinegar (5% acidity)

1 cup packed brown sugar

½ cup granulated sugar

1 medium yellow onion, finely diced

2 cloves garlic, minced

1 tbsp finely grated fresh ginger

1 tbsp mustard seeds

1 tsp ground cinnamon

1 tsp ground coriander

½ tsp ground cloves

½ tsp crushed red pepper flakes (optional)

½ tsp sea salt

½ tsp freshly ground black pepper

½ cup golden raisins or unsweetened dried cranberries (optional)

### INSTRUCTIONS

1   In a large stockpot, combine chopped apples, apple cider vinegar, brown sugar, granulated sugar, onion, garlic, ginger, mustard seeds, cinnamon, coriander, cloves, red pepper flakes (if using), salt, black pepper, and golden raisins or cranberries (if using).

2   Bring the mixture to a gentle boil over medium-high heat, then reduce heat and simmer, stirring occasionally, for 30 to 45 minutes, until the apples soften and the mixture thickens.

3   Using an immersion blender, purée the mixture until smooth. Alternatively, working in batches, transfer mixture to a blender and blend until smooth, then return it to the pot.

4   Simmer, stirring frequently, for 10 to 15 minutes, until the chutney reaches your desired thickness.

5   Meanwhile, prepare jars, bands, and lids for canning and keep warm (see page 33).

6   Ladle the hot chutney into prepared jars, leaving ½-inch headspace. Remove bubbles using a bubble remover (see page 34).

7   Using a clean, damp cloth or paper towel, wipe rims clean to ensure a proper seal. Place sterilized lids on jars. Then screw on bands and tighten just until fingertip-tight (see page 34).

8   Fill your water canner roughly three-quarters full of water. Bring to a boil over high heat.

9  Using a jar lifter, place jars in canner rack. Submerge rack in boiling water, ensuring jars are covered by at least 1 inch of water. (You may need to add a little extra boiling water.) Cover canner with lid and bring water to a rolling boil.

10  Process jars for 15 minutes (adjust for altitude, if needed; see page 198). At end of processing time, turn off heat and remove lid.

11  Once water has stopped boiling, use jar lifter to carefully remove jars, without tilting, and place on a towel.

12  Let jars cool, undisturbed, for 12 to 24 hours. Once completely cool, test the seals by gently pressing down on the center of the lids—they should not flex (see page 35).

## VARIATIONS

**Spicy Apple Chutney:** In Step 1, add ½ tsp cayenne pepper.

**Cranberry Apple Chutney:** In Step 1, add ½ cup unsweetened dried cranberries.

**Caramelized Apple Chutney:** In Step 1, sauté the onions and apples in 1 tbsp butter before adding other ingredients.

# PEACH SALSA

SUMMER/FALL | WATER BATH | YIELD: 5 (16-OZ) PINT JARS

*The first time I made peach salsa, it was for a backyard BBQ where we grilled citrus-marinated chicken and served it with a bright, fresh salsa. The combination of sweet peaches, a little heat, and a tangy lime finish was a game-changer. Now, it's my go-to for tacos, grilled fish, or even just scooped up with tortilla chips. Whether you love a classic fresh salsa or want to explore smoky or tropical variations, this recipe is endlessly adaptable.*

## INGREDIENTS

6 cups peeled, pitted, and diced fresh peaches (approx. 3 pounds)

1½ cups diced red bell pepper

1 cup diced red onion

1 to 2 jalapeños, finely diced (to taste)

½ cup chopped fresh cilantro, leaves and stems

½ cup apple cider vinegar (5% acidity)

¼ cup freshly squeezed lime juice

2 cloves garlic, minced

1 tbsp liquid honey (optional)

1 tsp ground cumin

½ tsp sea salt

## INSTRUCTIONS

1   In a large stockpot, combine peaches, bell pepper, red onion, jalapeños, cilantro, apple cider vinegar, lime juice, garlic, honey (if using), cumin, and salt. Bring the mixture to a gentle boil over medium-high heat, then reduce heat and simmer, stirring occasionally, for 5 to 10 minutes, until flavors meld.

2   Meanwhile, prepare jars, bands, and lids for canning and keep warm (see page 33).

3   Ladle the hot salsa into prepared jars, leaving ½-inch headspace. Remove bubbles using a bubble remover (see page 34).

4   Using a clean, damp cloth or paper towel, wipe rims clean to ensure a proper seal. Place sterilized lids on jars. Then screw on bands and tighten just until fingertip-tight (see page 34).

5   Fill your water canner roughly three-quarters full of water. Bring to a boil over high heat.

6   Using a jar lifter, place jars in canner rack. Submerge rack in boiling water, ensuring jars are covered by at least 1 inch of water. (You may need to add a little extra boiling water.) Cover canner with lid and bring water to a rolling boil.

7   Process jars for 15 minutes (adjust for altitude, if needed; see page 198). At end of processing time, turn off heat and remove lid.

8   Once water has stopped boiling, use jar lifter to carefully remove jars, without tilting, and place on a towel.

9   Let jars cool, undisturbed, for 12 to 24 hours. Once completely cool, test the seals by gently pressing down on the center of the lids—they should not flex (see page 35).

## VARIATIONS

**Tropical Peach Salsa:** In Step 1, stir in ½ cup diced mango or pineapple for a bright, fruity twist.

**Smoky Peach Salsa:** In Step 1, stir in ½ tsp smoked paprika for a deep, smoky flavor.

**Spicy Peach Salsa:** Swap jalapeños for habanero peppers for an extra kick.

# GARDEN VEGETABLE SAUCE

**SUMMER/FALL | PRESSURE CANNING | YIELD: 7 (32-OZ) QUART OR 14 (16-OZ) PINT JARS**

*A hearty, nutrient-rich vegetable sauce that captures the best flavors of summer and fall, this sauce is packed with zucchini, carrots, and fresh herbs. It's a versatile pantry staple, perfect for pasta, casseroles, roasted vegetables, or grain bowls. For added depth, roast red peppers before blending them into the sauce. Need a protein boost? Stir in cooked lentils or beans for a satisfying, plant-based meal.*

## INGREDIENTS

1 tbsp olive oil

2 cups finely chopped yellow onions

3 cups finely chopped carrots

2 cups diced red bell peppers

4 cloves garlic, minced

12 cups diced tomatoes (fresh or canned)

4 cups diced zucchini

1 tbsp dried basil

1 tbsp dried oregano

1 tsp dried thyme

1 tsp freshly ground black pepper

2 tsp sea salt

½ tsp crushed red pepper flakes (optional)

½ cup tomato paste

14 tbsp bottled lemon juice, divided

## INSTRUCTIONS

1   In a large stockpot, heat olive oil over medium heat. Add onions, carrots, and bell peppers, and sauté for 5 to 7 minutes, until softened. Stir in garlic and cook for another minute.

2   Stir in tomatoes, zucchini, basil, oregano, thyme, black pepper, salt, and red pepper flakes (if using). Bring the mixture to a gentle boil over medium-high heat, then reduce heat and simmer, stirring occasionally, for 30 to 45 minutes, until vegetables soften and sauce thickens.

3   Stir in tomato paste and continue simmering, stirring frequently, for an additional 10 to 15 minutes.

4   Meanwhile, prepare jars, bands, and lids for canning and keep warm (see page 49).

5   To each prepared jar, add bottled lemon juice (2 tbsp per quart or 1 tbsp per pint).

6   Ladle the hot garden vegetable sauce into jars, leaving 1-inch headspace. Remove bubbles using a bubble remover (see page 49).

7   Using a clean, damp cloth or paper towel, wipe rims clean. Place sterilized lids on jars. Then screw on bands and tighten just until fingertip-tight (see page 49).

8   Fill your pressure canner with 2 to 3 inches of water. (Check your model's manual for exact recommendations.)

9   Load jars onto rack in pressure canner, ensuring they don't touch. Affix canner lid and turn heat to high.

10  Once canner is steaming, allow it to vent steam for 10 minutes before closing the vent or adding the weight (see page 50).

11  Bring canner to the correct PSI for your model and altitude (see page 199). Process pints for 35 minutes and quarts for 40 minutes. (Start timer only when canner reaches correct pressure.)

12  Turn off heat and allow the canner to cool naturally. Do not remove the lid or regulator until the pressure gauge reads zero. Tilt the lid away from your face when opening the canner.

13  Use jar lifter to carefully remove jars, without tilting, and place on a towel.

14  Let jars cool, undisturbed, for 12 to 24 hours. Once completely cool, test the seals by gently pressing down on the center of the lids—they should not flex (see page 52).

---

## VARIATIONS

**Roasted Red Pepper Sauce:** In Step 2, roast and peel red peppers before adding them to the sauce.

**Protein-Packed Sauce:** Before serving, stir in cooked lentils or white beans for a heartier meal.

# MIXED PEPPER SAUCE

**SUMMER | PRESSURE CANNING | YIELD: 7 (32-OZ) QUART OR 14 (16-OZ) PINT JARS**

*The combination of roasted peppers, vine-ripened tomatoes, and a touch of spice makes this sauce incredibly versatile. I love using it as a grilled meat marinade, a bold pasta sauce, or drizzled over enchiladas for a smoky, rich depth of flavor. It's even delicious as a dipping sauce for crusty bread or a base for hearty stews.*

## INGREDIENTS

2 tbsp olive oil

2 cups diced yellow onions

3 cloves garlic, minced

6 cups peeled, cored, and chopped tomatoes

8 cups roasted bell peppers (red, yellow, or orange), peeled, seeded, and chopped (see Tip)

1 cup apple cider vinegar (5% acidity)

¼ cup freshly squeezed lime juice

¼ cup liquid honey (optional)

1 tbsp smoked paprika

1 tbsp ground cumin

1 tsp freshly ground black pepper

1 tsp sea salt

½ tsp crushed red pepper flakes (adjust for heat preference)

## INSTRUCTIONS

1   In a large stockpot, heat olive oil over medium heat. Add onions and garlic, and sauté for 5 minutes, until softened.

2   Stir in chopped tomatoes, roasted peppers, apple cider vinegar, lime juice, honey (if using), smoked paprika, cumin, black pepper, salt, and red pepper flakes. Bring the mixture to a gentle boil over medium-high heat, then reduce heat and simmer, stirring occasionally, for 30 to 45 minutes, until the sauce thickens slightly.

3   Using an immersion blender, purée the mixture until smooth. Alternatively, working in batches, transfer mixture to a blender and blend until smooth, then return it to the pot.

4   Simmer for another 10 minutes to allow flavors to meld.

5   Meanwhile, prepare jars, bands, and lids for canning and keep warm (see page 49).

6   Ladle the hot mixed pepper sauce into prepared jars, leaving 1-inch headspace. Remove bubbles using a bubble remover (see page 49).

7   Using a clean, damp cloth or paper towel, wipe rims clean to ensure a proper seal. Place sterilized lids on jars. Then screw on bands and tighten just until fingertip-tight (see page 49).

8   Fill your pressure canner with 2 to 3 inches of water. (Check your model's manual for exact recommendations.)

9   Load jars onto rack in pressure canner, ensuring they don't touch. Affix canner lid and turn heat to high.

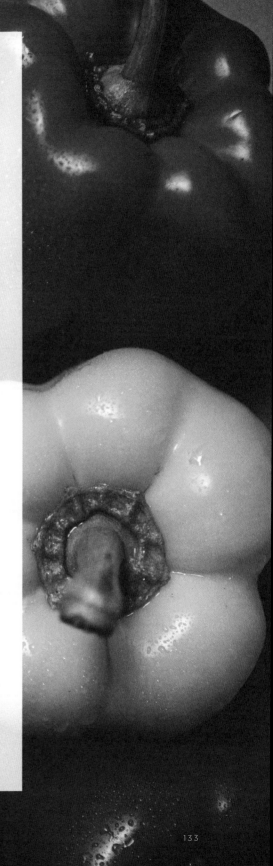

10　Once canner is steaming, allow it to vent steam for 10 minutes before closing the vent or adding the weight (see page 50).

11　Bring canner to the correct PSI for your model and altitude (see page 199). Process pints for 35 minutes and quarts for 40 minutes. (Start timer only when the canner reaches the correct pressure.)

12　Turn off heat and allow the canner to cool naturally. Do not remove the lid or regulator until the pressure gauge reads zero. Tilt the lid away from your face when opening the canner.

13　Use jar lifter to carefully remove jars, without tilting, and place on a towel.

14　Let jars cool, undisturbed, for 12 to 24 hours. Once completely cool, test the seals by gently pressing down on the center of the lids—they should not flex (see page 52).

## TIP

To roast the peppers: Preheat the oven to 450°F. Place peppers on a baking sheet, and roast for 20 to 25 minutes, turning occasionally, until skins are blistered and charred. Transfer to a bowl, cover with a clean towel, and let steam for 10 minutes. Peel, seed, and chop the peppers.

## VARIATIONS

**Chipotle Pepper Sauce:** In Step 2, add 1 tsp chipotle powder or roasted jalapeños.

**Herb-Infused Sauce:** In Step 3, before blending, stir in 1 tbsp chopped fresh oregano or basil for a bright, herbaceous twist.

**Sweeter Sauce:** Increase honey to ½ cup for a mild, caramelized sweetness.

# MUSHROOM SAUCE

YEAR-ROUND | PRESSURE CANNING | YIELD: 6 (16-OZ) PINT JARS

*This earthy, savory mushroom sauce is a perfect companion to pasta, rice, or roasted meats. Infused with rich tomatoes and red wine, it's a gourmet pantry essential for quick and elegant meals.*

## INGREDIENTS

10 pounds tomatoes, peeled, cored, and crushed

2 pounds fresh mushrooms, sliced

1 large yellow onion, diced

2 cloves garlic, minced

¼ cup olive oil

½ cup dry red wine

1 tbsp dried thyme

2 tsp sea salt

## INSTRUCTIONS

1  Peel tomatoes: In a large bowl, prepare an ice bath. Bring a large pot of water to a boil. Meanwhile, using a paring knife, cut a small X on the bottom of each tomato. Add tomatoes to water and boil (blanch) for 30 to 60 seconds. Using a slotted spoon or spider, transfer blanched tomatoes to the ice bath. Peel the skins, cut away any blemished areas, and crush tomatoes.

2  In a large skillet over medium heat, heat oil. Add mushrooms, onions, and garlic and sauté for 5 minutes, until softened and fragrant.

3  In a large stockpot, combine sautéed vegetables, crushed tomatoes, red wine, thyme, and salt. Simmer over medium heat for 30 minutes, stirring occasionally.

4  Meanwhile, prepare jars, bands, and lids for canning and keep warm (see page 49).

5  Ladle the hot mushroom sauce into prepared jars, leaving 1-inch headspace. Remove bubbles using a bubble remover (see page 49).

6  Using a clean, damp cloth or paper towel, wipe rims clean to ensure a proper seal. Place sterilized lids on jars. Then screw on bands and tighten just until fingertip-tight (see page 49).

7  Fill your pressure canner with 2 to 3 inches of water. (Check your model's manual for exact recommendations.)

8  Load jars onto rack in pressure canner, ensuring they don't touch. Affix canner lid and turn heat to high.

9  Once canner is steaming, allow it to vent steam for 10 minutes before closing the vent or adding the weight (see page 50).

10 Bring canner to the correct PSI for your model and altitude (see page 199). Process pints for 75 minutes. (Start timer only when the canner reaches the correct pressure.)

11 Turn off heat and allow the canner to cool naturally. Do not remove the lid or regulator until the pressure gauge reads zero. Tilt the lid away from your face when opening the canner.

12 Use jar lifter to carefully remove jars, without tilting, and place on a towel.

13 Let jars cool, undisturbed, for 12 to 24 hours. Once completely cool, test the seals by gently pressing down on the center of the lids—they should not flex (see page 52).

# MEAT SAUCE

**YEAR-ROUND | PRESSURE CANNING | YIELD: 4 (32-OZ) QUART OR 7 (16-OZ) PINT JARS**

*Growing up, Sunday dinners meant a big pot of simmering meat sauce, filling the house with rich, savory aromas. This classic meat sauce is thick, hearty, and packed with slow-cooked ground beef, tomatoes, and aromatic spices—perfect for pasta, casseroles, or lasagna.*

## INGREDIENTS

1 tbsp olive oil

3 pounds ground beef (or a mix of ground beef and Italian sausage)

1 medium yellow onion, diced

3 cloves garlic, minced

8 cups peeled, cored, and crushed tomatoes

1 cup tomato paste

1½ cups beef stock (page 148), visible fat skimmed if using homemade stock

½ cup dry red wine (optional)

¼ cup Worcestershire sauce

1 tbsp dried basil

1 tbsp dried oregano

1 tsp dried thyme

1 tsp freshly ground black pepper

2 tsp sea salt

½ tsp crushed red pepper flakes (optional)

## INSTRUCTIONS

1   In a large stockpot, heat olive oil over medium heat. Add ground beef, breaking it apart with a spoon, and cook until browned. Drain excess fat.

2   Add diced onion and garlic, and cook until softened, 3 to 5 minutes.

3   Stir in crushed tomatoes, tomato paste, beef stock, red wine (if using), and Worcestershire sauce. Add basil, oregano, thyme, black pepper, salt, and red pepper flakes (if using). Stir to combine. Bring the mixture to a gentle boil over medium-high heat, then reduce heat and simmer, stirring occasionally, for 45 minutes to 1 hour, until thickened slightly.

4   Meanwhile, prepare jars, bands, and lids for canning and keep warm (see page 49).

5   Ladle the hot meat sauce into prepared jars, leaving 1-inch headspace. Remove bubbles using a bubble remover (see page 49).

6   Using a clean, damp cloth or paper towel, wipe rims clean to ensure a proper seal.

7   Place sterilized lids on jars. Then screw on bands and tighten just until fingertip-tight (see page 49).

8   Fill the pressure canner with 2 to 3 inches of water. (Check your model's manual for exact recommendations.)

9   Load jars onto rack in pressure canner, ensuring they don't touch. Affix canner lid and turn heat to high.

10  Once canner is steaming, allow it to vent steam for 10 minutes before closing the vent or adding the weight (see page 50).

11  Bring canner to the correct PSI for your model and altitude (see page 199). Process pints for 75 minutes and quarts for 90 minutes. (Start timer only when the canner reaches the correct pressure.)

12  Turn off heat and allow the canner to cool naturally. Do not remove the lid or regulator until the pressure gauge reads zero. Tilt the lid away from your face when opening the canner.

13  Use jar lifter to carefully remove jars, without tilting, and place on a towel.

14  Let jars cool, undisturbed, for 12 to 24 hours. Once completely cool, test the seals by gently pressing down on the center of the lids—they should not flex (see page 52).

### VARIATIONS

**Sweet and Smoky Meat Sauce:** In Step 3, stir in ½ cup finely chopped roasted red peppers.

**Rich and Smoky Sauce:** In Step 3, add 1 tsp smoked paprika.

**Spicy Italian Sauce:** Use half ground beef and half spicy Italian sausage for extra heat.

CHAPTER 8

# BROTHS, STOCKS, AND SOUPS

| | | | | |
|---|---|---|---|---|
| Vegetable Broth | 140 | Potato Soup | 154 |
| Mushroom Broth | 142 | Tomato Soup | 156 |
| Fish Stock | 144 | Split Pea Soup | 158 |
| Chicken Stock | 146 | Black Bean Soup | 160 |
| Beef Stock | 148 | Lentil Soup | 162 |
| Vegetable Soup | 150 | Mixed Bean Soup | 164 |
| Minestrone Soup | 152 | Chicken Soup | 166 |

# MAKING FLAVORFUL STOCKS AND BROTHS

Creating a rich, flavorful stock or broth is the cornerstone of many preserved soups. (Stock is made from bones, and broth is made from meat or vegetables.) Follow these essential techniques for perfect results every time.

## INGREDIENT SELECTION

Choose high-quality ingredients for nutrient-rich stocks and broths. Use bones (chicken, beef, fish) with some meat attached, as well as fresh vegetables (onions, carrots, and celery). Avoid bitter or overpowering vegetables such as broccoli stems or cabbage.

## COOKING TIMES

Cooking times vary by stock type:

Chicken stock: 4 to 6 hours

Beef stock: 12 to 24 hours

Fish stock: 30 to 45 minutes

Longer cooking times for bone-based stocks allow collagen and nutrients to fully extract from the bones.

For vegetable broths, simmer gently for 1 to 2 hours to preserve delicate flavors.

## STRAINING METHODS

After simmering, strain the stock or broth through a fine-mesh sieve or cheesecloth, and discard solids. For clearer stock or broth, strain multiple times or use a fat separator to remove grease. A fat separator is a kitchen tool that separates fat from liquid by allowing it to rise to the top for easy removal.

## STORAGE GUIDELINES

Let stocks and broths cool completely before storing. Divide into manageable portions and refrigerate for up to 5 days, or freeze for up to 6 months.

If pressure canning, follow USDA guidelines for processing times and PSI levels.

# VEGETABLE BROTH

**YEAR-ROUND | PRESSURE CANNING | YIELD: 7 (32-OZ) QUART OR 14 (16-OZ) PINT JARS**

*Transform vegetable scraps into a nutrient-rich broth and reduce food waste (see Tip). The apple cider vinegar enhances nutrient extraction from the vegetables, making this a powerhouse addition to soups, stews, or even a warming beverage.*

### INGREDIENTS

8 cups vegetable scraps (e.g., carrot peels, celery ends, onion skins, leek tops, mushroom stems, and zucchini ends), cut into small pieces

2 cups chopped fresh vegetables (e.g., carrots, celery, onions, and parsley stems)

1 tbsp apple cider vinegar (5% acidity)

3 bay leaves

1 tsp whole black peppercorns

1 to 2 tsp sea salt (optional)

12 quarts water

### INSTRUCTIONS

1   In a large stockpot, combine vegetable scraps, fresh vegetables, apple cider vinegar, bay leaves, peppercorns, and salt (if using). Add water, ensuring it fully covers all ingredients.

2   Bring the mixture to a boil over medium-high heat, then reduce heat and gently simmer, uncovered, for 1 to 2 hours, stirring occasionally.

3   Meanwhile, prepare jars, bands, and lids for canning and keep warm (see page 49).

4   Using a slotted spoon or tongs, remove any large solids. Strain broth through a fine-mesh sieve or cheesecloth into a clean pot. Discard solids.

5   Ladle the hot broth into prepared jars, leaving 1-inch headspace.

6   Using a clean, damp cloth or paper towel, wipe rims clean. Place sterilized lids on jars. Then screw on bands and tighten just until fingertip-tight (see page 49).

7   Fill your pressure canner with 2 to 3 inches of water. (Check your model's manual for exact recommendations.)

8   Load jars onto rack in pressure canner, ensuring they don't touch. Affix canner lid and turn heat to high.

9   Once canner is steaming, allow it to vent steam for 10 minutes before closing the vent or adding the weight (see page 50).

10  Bring canner to the correct PSI for your model and altitude (see page 199). Process pints for 30 minutes and quarts for 35 minutes. (Start timer only when the canner reaches the correct pressure.)

11 Turn off heat and allow the canner to cool naturally. Do not remove the lid or regulator until the pressure gauge reads zero. Tilt the lid away from your face when opening the canner.

12 Use jar lifter to carefully remove jars, without tilting, and place on a towel.

13 Let jars cool, undisturbed, for 12 to 24 hours. Once completely cool, test the seals by gently pressing down on the center of the lids—they should not flex (see page 52).

---

TIP

Freeze vegetable scraps until you have enough to make a full batch of broth.

# MUSHROOM BROTH

**YEAR-ROUND | PRESSURE CANNING | YIELD: 7 (32-OZ) QUART OR 14 (16-OZ) PINT JARS**

*This umami-rich mushroom stock repurposes scraps and stems into a nutrient-dense, flavorful base perfect for soups, risottos, or sipping (see Tip).*

### INGREDIENTS

2 pounds assorted mushroom scraps (stems, tough caps, trimmings)

2 cups diced carrots

2 cups diced celery

2 cups diced yellow onions

¼ cup apple cider vinegar (5% acidity)

2 to 3 sprigs fresh thyme or 1 tsp dried thyme

3 bay leaves

1 tsp whole black peppercorns

1 to 2 tsp sea salt (to taste; optional)

12 quarts water

### INSTRUCTIONS

1   In a large stockpot, combine mushroom scraps, fresh vegetables, apple cider vinegar, thyme, bay leaves, peppercorns, and salt (if using). Add water, ensuring it fully covers ingredients.

2   Bring to a boil over medium-high heat, then reduce heat and gently simmer, uncovered, for 1 to 2 hours, stirring occasionally.

3   Meanwhile, prepare jars, bands, and lids for canning and keep warm (see page 49).

4   Using a slotted spoon or tongs, remove any large solids. Strain broth through a fine-mesh sieve or cheesecloth into a clean pot. Discard solids.

5   Ladle the hot broth into prepared jars, leaving 1-inch headspace.

6   Using a clean, damp cloth or paper towel, wipe rims clean. Place sterilized lids on jars. Then screw on bands and tighten just until fingertip-tight (see page 49).

7   Fill your pressure canner with 2 to 3 inches of water. (Check your model's manual for exact recommendations.)

8   Load jars onto rack in pressure canner, ensuring they don't touch. Affix canner lid and turn heat to high.

9   Once canner is steaming, allow it to vent steam for 10 minutes before closing the vent or adding the weight (see page 50).

10  Bring canner to the correct PSI for your model and altitude (see page 199). Process pints for 30 minutes and quarts for 35 minutes. (Start timer only when canner reaches correct pressure.)

11 Turn off heat and allow the canner to cool naturally. Do not remove the lid or regulator until the pressure gauge reads zero. Tilt the lid away from your face when opening the canner.

12 Use jar lifter to carefully remove jars, without tilting, and place on a towel.

13 Let jars cool, undisturbed, for 12 to 24 hours. Once completely cool, test the seals by gently pressing down on the center of the lids—they should not flex (see page 52).

TIP

Freeze mushroom scraps until you accumulate enough for a full batch of broth.

# FISH STOCK

**YEAR-ROUND | PRESSURE CANNING | YIELD: 7 (32-OZ) QUART OR 14 (16-OZ) PINT JARS**

*Fish stock is packed with gelatin, iodine, and essential minerals. Using fish heads, bones, and scraps ensures a nutrient-rich, sustainable broth perfect for seafood chowders, risottos, and soups.*

## INGREDIENTS

3 to 4 pounds fish heads, bones, and scraps (from nonoily fish like cod, sole, haddock, or halibut)

2 cups diced carrots

2 cups diced celery

2 cups diced onions

¼ cup apple cider vinegar (5% acidity)

2 to 3 bay leaves

1 tsp whole black peppercorns

1 to 2 tsp sea salt (to taste; optional)

12 quarts water

## INSTRUCTIONS

1   In a large stockpot, combine fish (heads, bones, and scraps), fresh vegetables, apple cider vinegar, bay leaves, peppercorns, and salt (if using). Add water, ensuring it fully covers ingredients.

2   Bring to a boil over medium-high heat, then reduce heat and gently simmer, uncovered, for 1 to 2 hours, stirring occasionally.

3   Meanwhile, prepare jars, bands, and lids for canning and keep warm (see page 49).

4   Using a slotted spoon or tongs, remove any large solids. Strain stock through a fine-mesh sieve or cheesecloth into a clean pot. Discard solids.

5   Ladle the hot stock into prepared jars, leaving 1-inch headspace.

6   Using a clean, damp cloth or paper towel, wipe rims clean. Place sterilized lids on jars. Then screw on bands and tighten just until fingertip-tight (see page 49).

7   Fill your pressure canner with 2 to 3 inches of water. (Check your model's manual for exact recommendations.)

8   Load jars onto rack in pressure canner, ensuring they don't touch. Affix canner lid and turn heat to high.

9   Once canner is steaming, allow it to vent steam for 10 minutes before closing the vent or adding the weight (see page 50).

10   Bring canner to the correct PSI for your model and altitude (see page 199). Process pints for 30 minutes and quarts for 35 minutes. (Start timer only when canner reaches correct pressure.)

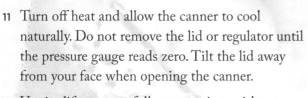

11 Turn off heat and allow the canner to cool naturally. Do not remove the lid or regulator until the pressure gauge reads zero. Tilt the lid away from your face when opening the canner.

12 Use jar lifter to carefully remove jars, without tilting, and place on a towel.

13 Let jars cool, undisturbed, for 12 to 24 hours. Once completely cool, test the seals by gently pressing down on the center of the lids—they should not flex (see page 52).

---

### VARIATION

**For an herbal boost:** In Step 2, add ¼ cup chopped fresh parsley or 2 tbsp chopped fresh dill during the last 10 minutes of simmering.

# CHICKEN STOCK

**YEAR-ROUND | PRESSURE CANNING | YIELD: 7 (32-OZ) QUART OR 14 (16-OZ) PINT JARS**

*Packed with collagen and minerals, this rich, flavorful stock is made from chicken carcasses and feet, delivering deep nutrition. (The addition of chicken feet boosts collagen levels in the broth.) This is a perfect base for soups and stews, or a satisfying sipping broth all on its own.*

## INGREDIENTS

2 to 3 chicken carcasses (see Tip)

1 to 2 pounds chicken feet

2 cups diced carrots

2 cups diced celery

2 cups diced yellow onions

¼ cup apple cider vinegar (5% acidity)

2 to 3 bay leaves

1 tsp whole black peppercorns

½ to 2 tsp sea salt (to taste; optional)

12 quarts water

## INSTRUCTIONS

1  Preheat oven to 400°F.

2  In a large roasting pan, roast chicken carcasses for 30 to 40 minutes, or until golden brown. (You may need to do this in batches.) Transfer to a large stockpot.

3  To the stockpot, add feet scraps, fresh vegetables, apple cider vinegar, bay leaves, peppercorns, and salt (if using). Add water, ensuring it fully covers all ingredients.

4  Bring to a boil over medium-high heat, then reduce heat and gently simmer, uncovered, for 1 to 2 hours, stirring occasionally.

5  Meanwhile, prepare jars, bands, and lids for canning and keep warm (see page 49).

6  Using a slotted spoon or tongs, remove any large solids. Strain stock through a fine-mesh sieve or cheesecloth into a clean pot. Discard solids.

7  Ladle the hot stock into prepared jars, leaving 1-inch headspace.

8  Using a clean, damp cloth or paper towel, wipe rims clean. Place sterilized lids on jars. Then screw on bands and tighten just until fingertip-tight (see page 49).

9  Fill your pressure canner with 2 to 3 inches of water. (Check your model's manual for exact recommendations.)

10  Load jars onto rack in pressure canner, ensuring they don't touch. Affix canner lid and turn heat to high.

11 Once canner is steaming, allow it to vent steam for 10 minutes before closing the vent or adding the weight (see page 50).

12 Bring canner to the correct PSI for your model and altitude (see page 199). Process pints for 20 minutes and quarts for 25 minutes. (Start timer only when canner reaches correct pressure.)

13 Turn off heat and allow the canner to cool naturally. Do not remove the lid or regulator until the pressure gauge reads zero. Tilt the lid away from your face when opening the canner.

14 Use jar lifter to carefully remove jars, without tilting, and place on a towel.

15 Let jars cool, undisturbed, for 12 to 24 hours. Once completely cool, test the seals by gently pressing down on the center of the lids—they should not flex (see page 52).

---

**VARIATION**

**For herbal depth of flavor:** In Step 2, add 4 sprigs of fresh thyme or ¼ cup chopped fresh parsley during the last hour of simmering.

# BEEF STOCK

**YEAR-ROUND | PRESSURE CANNING | YIELD: 7 (32-OZ) QUART OR 14 (16-OZ) PINT JARS**

*This rich, flavorful beef stock is a versatile pantry staple for soups, stews, and sauces. Roasting the bones enhances depth of flavor, while apple cider vinegar ensures maximum mineral extraction from the vegetables.*

### INGREDIENTS

5 to 6 pounds beef bones (marrow bones, knuckles, or joints)

¼ cup apple cider vinegar (5% acidity)

12 quarts water

2 cups diced carrots

2 cups diced celery

2 cups diced yellow onions

2 to 3 sprigs fresh thyme or 1 tsp dried thyme

2 to 3 bay leaves

1 tsp whole black peppercorns

1 tsp sea salt (optional)

### INSTRUCTIONS

1. Preheat oven to 425°F.

2. Arrange beef bones in a single layer on a roasting pan. Roast for 40 to 45 minutes, turning halfway through, until deeply browned and aromatic. Transfer roasted bones to a large stockpot.

3. Add apple cider vinegar and water, ensuring bones are fully covered. Let sit for 30 to 60 minutes. (This helps break down the collagen and extract minerals, resulting in a more nutrient-dense and gelatin-rich broth.)

4. To the stockpot, add fresh vegetables, thyme, bay leaves, peppercorns, and salt (if using). Add additional water to fully cover ingredients. Bring to a boil over medium-high heat, then reduce heat and gently simmer for 12 to 24 hours, adding water if needed to ensure ingredients are well covered and skimming off foam and impurities for the first 30 minutes.

5. Using a slotted spoon or tongs, remove any large solids. Strain stock through a fine-mesh sieve or cheesecloth into a clean pot. Discard solids. Allow it to cool slightly and skim off excess fat if desired.

6. Meanwhile, prepare jars, bands, and lids for canning and keep warm (see page 49).

7. Ladle stock into prepared jars, leaving 1-inch headspace.

8. Using a clean, damp cloth or paper towel, wipe rims clean. Place sterilized lids on jars. Then screw on bands and tighten just until fingertip-tight (see page 49).

9   Fill your pressure canner with 2 to 3 inches of water. (Check your model's manual for exact recommendations.)

10  Load jars onto rack in pressure canner, ensuring they don't touch. Affix canner lid and turn heat to high.

11  Once canner is steaming, allow it to vent steam for 10 minutes before closing the vent or adding the weight (see page 50).

12  Bring canner to the correct PSI for your model and altitude (see page 199). Process pints for 20 minutes and quarts for 25 minutes. (Start timer only when canner reaches correct pressure.)

13  Turn off heat and allow the canner to cool naturally. Do not remove the lid or regulator until the pressure gauge reads zero. Tilt the lid away from your face when opening the canner.

14  Use jar lifter to carefully remove jars, without tilting, and place on a towel.

15  Let jars cool, undisturbed, for 12 to 24 hours. Once completely cool, test the seals by gently pressing down on the center of the lids—they should not flex (see page 52).

---

## VARIATION

**For extra depth of flavor:** In Step 4, add ¼ cup chopped fresh parsley during the last hour of simmering.

# VEGETABLE SOUP

**YEAR-ROUND | PRESSURE CANNING | YIELD: 7 (32-OZ) QUART OR 14 (16-OZ) PINT JARS**

*This nutrient-dense vegetable soup is made with fresh seasonal vegetables and a rich homemade stock, creating a wholesome, long-lasting meal. Perfect for quick lunches, hearty dinners, or a comforting bowl on a chilly day.*

## INGREDIENTS

2 quarts vegetable broth (page 140) or chicken stock (page 146), visible fat skimmed if using homemade stock

3 cups diced carrots

3 cups diced celery

2 cups diced potatoes

2 cups trimmed and chopped green beans

1 cup corn kernels (fresh or frozen)

1 cup diced zucchini

2 cups diced tomatoes (fresh or canned)

1 tbsp apple cider vinegar (5% acidity) (optional)

2 tsp sea salt (optional)

1 tsp dried thyme

1 tsp dried oregano

½ tsp freshly ground black pepper

## INSTRUCTIONS

1   In a large stockpot, combine vegetable broth or chicken stock with the carrots, celery, potatoes, green beans, corn, zucchini, and tomatoes.

2   Add apple cider vinegar and salt (if using), thyme, oregano, and black pepper. Stir to combine.

3   Bring the soup to a gentle boil over medium-high heat, then reduce heat and simmer for 10 minutes. (This helps soften the vegetables slightly while maintaining their texture during canning.)

4   Meanwhile, prepare jars, bands, and lids for canning and keep warm (see page 49).

5   Ladle the hot soup into prepared jars, leaving 1-inch headspace. (Ensure each jar gets an even mix of vegetables and broth.) Remove bubbles using a bubble remover (see page 49).

6   Using a clean, damp cloth or paper towel, wipe rims clean. Place sterilized lids on jars. Then screw on bands and tighten just until fingertip-tight (see page 49).

7   Fill your pressure canner with 2 to 3 inches of water. (Check your model's manual for exact recommendations.)

8   Load jars onto rack in pressure canner, ensuring they don't touch. Affix canner lid and turn heat to high.

9 Once canner is steaming, allow it to vent steam for 10 minutes before closing the vent or adding the weight (see page 50).

10 Bring canner to the correct PSI for your model and altitude (see page 199). Process pints for 75 minutes and quarts for 90 minutes. (Start timer only when canner reaches correct pressure.)

11 Turn off heat and allow the canner to cool naturally. Do not remove the lid or regulator until the pressure gauge reads zero. Tilt the lid away from your face when opening the canner.

12 Use jar lifter to carefully remove jars, without tilting, and place on a towel.

13 Let jars cool, undisturbed, for 12 to 24 hours. Once completely cool, test the seals by gently pressing down on the center of the lids—they should not flex (see page 52).

---

TIP

For extra flavor, add 2 tbsp finely chopped parsley leaves and a drizzle of olive oil after reheating. This preserves the delicate herbal notes and enhances nutrient content.

# MINESTRONE SOUP

**YEAR-ROUND | PRESSURE CANNING | YIELD: 7 (32-OZ) QUART OR 14 (16-OZ) PINT JARS**

*This hearty and nutrient-dense minestrone soup is packed with vegetables and beans, making it a comforting and satisfying meal. Soaking the beans overnight in water and apple cider vinegar helps break down the phytic acid, which can improve digestion and nutrient absorption. This extra step also ensures that the beans fully hydrate before canning, which is essential for safe preservation.*

## INGREDIENTS

1 cup dried cannellini beans, rinsed and drained

¼ cup plus 1 tbsp apple cider vinegar (5% acidity), divided

2 quarts beef stock (page 148) or chicken stock (page 146), visible fat skimmed if homemade

3 cups diced carrots

3 cups diced celery

3 cups diced yellow onions

3 cups diced zucchini

2 cups shredded green cabbage

2 cups diced tomatoes (fresh or canned)

1 cup diced peeled potatoes

1 cup chopped green beans

2 tsp sea salt (optional)

1 tsp dried oregano

1 tsp dried basil

½ tsp freshly ground black pepper

## INSTRUCTIONS

1   Soak beans: In a large pot, cover dried beans with water. Stir in apple cider vinegar and let soak for 12 to 18 hours.

2   Precook beans: Drain beans and rinse well. Return beans to the pot and cover with fresh cold water. Place over medium-high heat and bring to a boil. Reduce heat and simmer for 30 minutes. Drain beans and set aside.

3   In a large stockpot, combine stock, partially cooked beans, vegetables, apple cider vinegar, salt (if using), oregano, basil, and black pepper. Bring to a gentle boil over medium-high heat, then reduce heat and simmer for 10 minutes, or until vegetables are firm but slightly softened.

4   Meanwhile, prepare jars, bands, and lids for canning and keep warm (see page 49).

5   Ladle the hot soup into prepared jars, leaving 1-inch headspace. Ensure each jar gets an even mix of vegetables, beans, and stock. Remove bubbles using a bubble remover (see page 49).

6   Using a clean, damp cloth or paper towel, wipe rims clean. Place sterilized lids on jars. Then screw on bands and tighten just until fingertip-tight (see page 49).

7   Fill your pressure canner with 2 to 3 inches of water. (Check your model's manual for exact recommendations.)

8   Load jars onto rack in pressure canner, ensuring they don't touch. Affix canner lid and turn heat to high.

9   Once canner is steaming, allow it to vent steam for 10 minutes before closing the vent or adding the weight (see page 50).

10  Bring canner to the correct PSI for your model and altitude (see page 199). Process pints for 75 minutes and quarts for 90 minutes. (Start timer only when canner reaches correct pressure.)

11  Turn off heat and allow the canner to cool naturally. Do not remove the lid or regulator until the pressure gauge reads zero. Tilt the lid away from your face when opening the canner.

12  Use jar lifter to carefully remove jars, without tilting, and place on a towel.

13  Let jars cool, undisturbed, for 12 to 24 hours. Once completely cool, test the seals by gently pressing down on the center of the lids—they should not flex (see page 52).

## TIPS

Draining the precooked beans ensures proper texture and prevents excessive starchiness in the soup.

For a heartier meal, stir in cooked pasta or rice when reheating.

# POTATO SOUP

**YEAR-ROUND | PRESSURE CANNING | YIELD: 7 (32-OZ) QUART OR 14 (16-OZ) PINT JARS**

*Growing up, potato soup was a cold-weather staple in my family—thick, creamy, and deeply comforting. But when it comes to canning, you must avoid adding cream, milk, or thickeners before processing (see page 44). This recipe gives you a simple, flavorful base that's perfect for long-term storage. When you're ready to serve, stir in cream, milk, or a thickener while reheating to achieve that rich, velvety texture we all love.*

### INGREDIENTS

2 quarts vegetable broth (page 140) or chicken stock (page 146), visible fat skimmed if using homemade stock

5 cups diced potatoes

3 cups diced celery

3 cups diced yellow onions

2 cups diced carrots

1 tsp sea salt (optional)

1 tsp dried thyme

½ tsp freshly ground black pepper

### INSTRUCTIONS

1   In a large stockpot, combine broth or stock, potatoes, celery, onions, carrots, salt (if using), thyme, and black pepper. Bring to a gentle boil over medium-high heat, then reduce heat and simmer for 10 minutes, or until vegetables are firm but slightly softened. (This precooking step helps maintain texture during the canning process.)

2   Meanwhile, prepare jars, bands, and lids for canning and keep warm (see page 49).

3   Ladle the hot soup into prepared jars, leaving 1-inch headspace. Ensure each jar gets an even mix of vegetables and broth. Remove bubbles using a bubble remover (see page 49).

4   Using a clean, damp cloth or paper towel, wipe rims clean. Place sterilized lids on jars. Then screw on bands and tighten just until fingertip-tight (see page 49).

5   Fill your pressure canner with 2 to 3 inches of water. (Check your model's manual for exact recommendations.)

6   Load jars onto rack in pressure canner, ensuring they don't touch. Affix canner lid and turn heat to high.

7   Once canner is steaming, allow it to vent steam for 10 minutes before closing the vent or adding the weight (see page 50).

8   Bring canner to the correct PSI for your model and altitude (see page 199). Process pints for 75 minutes and quarts for 90 minutes. (Start timer only when the canner reaches the correct pressure.)

9 Turn off heat and allow the canner to cool naturally. Do not remove the lid or regulator until the pressure gauge reads zero. Tilt the lid away from your face when opening the canner.

10 Use jar lifter to carefully remove jars, without tilting, and place on a towel.

11 Let jars cool, undisturbed, for 12 to 24 hours. Once completely cool, test the seals by gently pressing down on the center of the lids—they should not flex (see page 52).

## TIPS

Avoid cream or dairy products: Add cream, milk, or butter only after reheating (this prevents curdling during canning).

Avoid thickeners: Do not add flour or cornstarch before canning (adjust thickness after reheating).

For added flavor, garnish with fresh chives, parsley, or crumbled bacon.

Once you open the jar, purée the soup or leave whole, based on texture desired.

# TOMATO SOUP

**LATE SUMMER/FALL | PRESSURE CANNING | YIELD: 7 (32-OZ) QUART OR 14 (16-OZ) PINT JARS**

*Rich and comforting, this recipe combines ripe tomatoes with loads of aromatic vegetables. After reheating, stir in cream or milk for a creamy tomato soup. Garnish with fresh basil and a drizzle of olive oil. Serve with grilled cheese sandwiches or croutons for a classic, cozy meal.*

## INGREDIENTS

2 quarts vegetable broth (page 140) or chicken stock (page 146), visible fat skimmed if using homemade stock

8 cups peeled, cored, and chopped tomatoes (see Tips)

3 cups diced yellow onions

2 cups diced celery

2 cups diced carrots

3 cloves garlic, minced

1 tbsp apple cider vinegar (5% acidity) (optional)

2 tsp sea salt (optional)

1 tsp dried basil

1 tsp dried oregano

½ tsp freshly ground black pepper

## INSTRUCTIONS

1   In a large stockpot, combine broth or stock, tomatoes, onions, celery, carrots, garlic, apple cider vinegar (if using), salt (if using), basil, oregano, and black pepper. Bring to a gentle boil over medium-high heat, then reduce heat and simmer, uncovered, for 10 to 15 minutes, stirring occasionally. (This softens the vegetables and allows the flavors to meld.)

2   Meanwhile, prepare jars, bands, and lids for canning and keep warm (see page 49).

3   Ladle the hot soup into prepared jars, leaving 1-inch headspace. Remove bubbles using a bubble remover (see page 49).

4   Using a clean, damp cloth or paper towel, wipe rims clean. Place sterilized lids on jars. Then screw on bands and tighten just until fingertip-tight (see page 49).

5   Fill your pressure canner with 2 to 3 inches of water. (Check your model's manual for exact recommendations.)

6   Load jars onto rack in pressure canner, ensuring they don't touch. Affix canner lid and turn heat to high.

7   Once canner is steaming, allow it to vent steam for 10 minutes before closing the vent or adding the weight (see page 50).

8   Bring canner to the correct PSI for your model and altitude (see page 199). Process pints for 20 minutes and quarts for 25 minutes. (Start timer only when canner reaches correct pressure.)

9  Turn off heat and allow the canner to cool naturally. Do not remove the lid or regulator until the pressure gauge reads zero. Tilt the lid away from your face when opening the canner.

10  Use jar lifter to carefully remove jars, without tilting, and place on a towel.

11  Let jars cool, undisturbed, for 12 to 24 hours. Once completely cool, test the seals by gently pressing down on the center of the lids—they should not flex (see page 52).

---

## TIPS

To peel tomatoes, blanch them in boiling water for 30 seconds, transfer to an ice bath, and slip off the skins. Core and chop the peeled tomatoes before adding them to the soup in Step 1.

Avoid dairy products: Add cream, milk, or other dairy products after opening and reheating to prevent curdling.

Avoid thickeners: Do not add thickeners before canning. If a thicker soup is desired, use a flour or cornstarch slurry after reheating.

For a smooth soup, use an immersion blender or transfer batches to a countertop blender to purée. Leave some texture, if preferred.

# SPLIT PEA SOUP

**YEAR-ROUND | PRESSURE CANNING | YIELD: 7 (32-OZ) QUART OR 14 (16-OZ) PINT JARS**

*This hearty split pea soup combines homemade broth, fresh vegetables, and naturally thickening split peas. Safe pressure canning techniques ensure a delicious, shelf-stable soup that's ready when you are.*

## INGREDIENTS

2 quarts vegetable broth (page 140) or chicken stock (page 146), visible fat skimmed if using homemade stock

2 cups dried split peas, rinsed and drained

3 cups diced carrots

3 cups diced celery

2 cups diced yellow onions

2 cups diced peeled potatoes

2 tsp sea salt (optional)

1 tsp dried thyme

½ tsp freshly ground black pepper

## INSTRUCTIONS

1  In a large stockpot, combine broth, split peas, carrots, celery, onions, potatoes, salt (if using), thyme, and black pepper. Bring to a gentle boil over medium-high heat, then reduce heat and simmer for 10 minutes. (The split peas will continue thickening during canning.)

2  Meanwhile, prepare jars, bands, and lids for canning and keep warm (see page 49).

3  Ladle the hot soup into prepared jars, leaving 1-inch headspace. Remove bubbles using a bubble remover (see page 49).

4  Using a clean, damp cloth or paper towel, wipe rims clean. Place sterilized lids on jars. Then screw on bands and tighten just until fingertip-tight (see page 49).

5  Fill your pressure canner with 2 to 3 inches of water. (Check your model's manual for exact recommendations.)

6  Load jars onto rack in pressure canner, ensuring they don't touch. Affix canner lid and turn heat to high.

7  Once canner is steaming, allow it to vent steam for 10 minutes before closing the vent or adding the weight (see page 50).

8  Bring canner to the correct PSI for your model and altitude (see page 199). Process pints for 75 minutes and quarts for 90 minutes. (Start timer only when canner reaches correct pressure.)

9  Turn off heat and allow the canner to cool naturally. Do not remove the lid or regulator until the pressure gauge reads zero. Tilt the lid away from your face when opening the canner.

10  Use jar lifter to carefully remove jars, without tilting, and place on a towel.

11 Let jars cool, undisturbed, for 12 to 24 hours. Once completely cool, test the seals by gently pressing down on the center of the lids—they should not flex (see page 52).

## TIPS

Ensure fat has been fully skimmed from broth or stock before canning to prevent spoilage.

Avoid thickeners: Split peas naturally thicken the soup, making additional starches unnecessary.

## VARIATION

For a heartier soup, stir in cooked ham or bacon after reheating.

# BLACK BEAN SOUP

**YEAR-ROUND | PRESSURE CANNING | YIELD: 7 (32-OZ) QUART OR 14 (16-OZ) PINT JARS**

*Whether served as a hearty standalone meal, a base for tacos, or blended into a creamy, restaurant-style soup, this recipe never disappoints. Just pop open a jar, reheat, and enjoy with a squeeze of lime, fresh cilantro, and crumbled queso fresco. If you love a little heat, stir in chipotle peppers or a dash of smoked paprika before serving for an extra kick.*

### INGREDIENTS

2 quarts vegetable broth (page 140) or chicken stock (page 146), visible fat skimmed if using homemade stock

2 cups dried black beans, soaked overnight and partially cooked (see Tips)

3 cups diced yellow onions

2 cups diced celery

2 cups diced carrots

1 cup diced bell peppers (red or green)

3 cloves garlic, minced

1 tsp sea salt (optional)

1 tsp ground cumin

1 tsp smoked paprika

½ tsp freshly ground black pepper

¼ tsp cayenne pepper (optional)

### INSTRUCTIONS

1 In a large stockpot, combine broth, prepared black beans, onions, celery, carrots, bell peppers, garlic, salt (if using), cumin, paprika, black pepper, and cayenne (if using). Bring to a gentle boil over medium-high heat, then reduce heat and simmer for 10 minutes.

2 Meanwhile, prepare jars, bands, and lids for canning and keep warm (see page 49).

3 Ladle the hot soup into prepared jars, leaving 1-inch headspace. (This allows for proper expansion during canning.) Remove bubbles using a bubble remover (see page 49).

4 Using a clean, damp cloth or paper towel, wipe rims clean. Place sterilized lids on jars. Then screw on bands and tighten just until fingertip-tight (see page 49).

5 Fill your pressure canner with 2 to 3 inches of water. (Check your model's manual for exact recommendations.)

6 Load jars onto rack in pressure canner, ensuring they don't touch. Affix canner lid and turn heat to high.

7 Once canner is steaming, allow it to vent steam for 10 minutes before closing the vent or adding the weight (see page 50).

8  Bring canner to the correct PSI for your model and altitude (see page 199). Process pints for 75 minutes and quarts for 90 minutes. (Start timer only when canner reaches correct pressure.)

9  Turn off heat and allow the canner to cool naturally. Do not remove the lid or regulator until the pressure gauge reads zero. Tilt the lid away from your face when opening the canner.

10  Use jar lifter to carefully remove jars, without tilting, and place on a towel.

11  Let jars cool, undisturbed, for 12 to 24 hours. Once completely cool, test the seals by gently pressing down on the center of the lids—they should not flex (see page 52).

---

### TIPS

To soak dried black beans, place them in a large pot, cover in plenty of cold water, and set aside for 12 to 18 hours. Adding 1 tablespoon of apple cider vinegar to the soaking water will help improve their digestibility.

Avoid fats: Do not add fats or oils during the canning process. Add them after reheating, if desired.

Avoid thickeners: For a thicker soup, mash some beans, or add a flour or cornstarch slurry after reheating.

# LENTIL SOUP

**YEAR-ROUND | PRESSURE CANNING | YIELD: 7 (32-OZ) QUART OR 14 (16-OZ) PINT JARS**

*This hearty, protein-rich lentil soup is packed with nutrient-dense vegetables and warming spices. Enhance nutrition by stirring in fresh spinach or kale after reheating, or add a squeeze of lemon juice and garnish with fresh parsley for brightness. Serve with crusty bread or over rice for a satisfying meal.*

## INGREDIENTS

2 quarts vegetable broth (page 140) or chicken stock (page 146), visible fat skimmed if using homemade stock

2 cups dried lentils, rinsed and drained

3 cups diced carrots

3 cups diced celery

2 cups diced yellow onions

2 cups diced peeled potatoes

3 cloves garlic, minced

1 tsp sea salt (optional)

1 tsp ground cumin

1 tsp smoked paprika

½ tsp freshly ground black pepper

¼ tsp cayenne pepper (optional)

## INSTRUCTIONS

1   In a large stockpot, combine broth, lentils, vegetables, garlic, salt (if using), cumin, paprika, black pepper, and cayenne (if using). Bring to a gentle boil over medium-high heat, then reduce heat and simmer for 10 to 15 minutes, or until vegetables are slightly softened but still firm. (The lentils will continue to cook during canning.)

2   Meanwhile, prepare jars, bands, and lids for canning and keep warm (see page 49).

3   Ladle the hot soup into prepared jars, leaving 1-inch headspace. Remove bubbles using a bubble remover (see page 49).

4   Using a clean, damp cloth or paper towel, wipe rims clean. Place sterilized lids on jars. Then screw on bands and tighten just until fingertip-tight (see page 49).

5   Fill your pressure canner with 2 to 3 inches of water. (Check your model's manual for exact recommendations.)

6   Load jars onto rack in pressure canner, ensuring they don't touch. Affix canner lid and turn heat to high.

7   Once canner is steaming, allow it to vent steam for 10 minutes before closing the vent or adding the weight (see page 50).

8   Bring canner to the correct PSI for your model and altitude (see page 199). Process pints for 75 minutes and quarts for 90 minutes. (Start timer only when canner reaches correct pressure.)

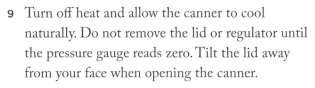

9   Turn off heat and allow the canner to cool naturally. Do not remove the lid or regulator until the pressure gauge reads zero. Tilt the lid away from your face when opening the canner.

10  Use jar lifter to carefully remove jars, without tilting, and place on a towel.

11  Let jars cool, undisturbed, for 12 to 24 hours. Once completely cool, test the seals by gently pressing down on the center of the lids—they should not flex (see page 52).

### TIPS

Avoid fats: Do not add fats or oils during the canning process. Add them after reheating, if desired.

Avoid thickeners: For a thicker soup, mash some lentils or add a flour or cornstarch slurry after reheating.

# MIXED BEAN SOUP

**YEAR-ROUND | PRESSURE CANNING | YIELD: 7 (32-OZ) QUART OR 14 (16-OZ) PINT JARS**

*This protein-rich, fiber-filled mixed bean soup is both flavorful and filling—a pantry staple perfect for easy meals. And you can customize it with your favorite beans or whatever you have on hand. You'll need to begin this recipe the day before you plan on canning to allow enough time to soak the beans.*

## INGREDIENTS

1 cup dried kidney beans

1 cup dried navy beans

1 cup dried pinto beans

2 quarts beef stock (page 148) or chicken stock (page 146), visible fat skimmed if homemade

3 cups diced carrots

3 cups diced celery

3 cups diced yellow onions

2 cups diced tomatoes (fresh or canned)

1 cup diced peeled potatoes

2 tsp sea salt (optional)

1 tsp dried oregano

1 tsp dried thyme

½ tsp freshly ground black pepper

## INSTRUCTIONS

1   Prepare beans: Soak kidney, navy, and pinto beans in water for 12 to 18 hours. Drain, rinse, and add to a stockpot. Cover with fresh water and boil for 30 minutes to ensure proper hydration for safe canning. Drain and set aside.

2   In a large stockpot, combine stock, precooked beans, carrots, celery, onions, tomatoes, potatoes, salt (if using), oregano, thyme, and black pepper. Stir to combine. Bring to a gentle boil over medium-high heat, then reduce heat and simmer for 10 minutes, allowing the flavors to meld.

3   Meanwhile, prepare jars, bands, and lids for canning and keep warm (see page 49).

4   Ladle the hot soup into prepared jars, leaving 1-inch headspace. Ensure an even distribution of beans, vegetables, and stock. Remove bubbles using a bubble remover (see page 49).

5   Using a clean, damp cloth or paper towel, wipe rims clean. Place sterilized lids on jars. Then screw on bands and tighten just until fingertip-tight (see page 49).

6   Fill your pressure canner with 2 to 3 inches of water. (Check your model's manual for exact recommendations.)

7   Load jars onto rack in pressure canner, ensuring they don't touch. Affix canner lid and turn heat to high.

8   Once canner is steaming, allow it to vent steam for 10 minutes before closing the vent or adding the weight (see page 50).

9  Bring canner to the correct PSI for your model and altitude (see page 199). Process pints for 75 minutes and quarts for 90 minutes. (Start timer only when canner reaches correct pressure.)

10 Turn off heat and allow the canner to cool naturally. Do not remove the lid or regulator until the pressure gauge reads zero. Tilt the lid away from your face when opening the canner.

11 Use jar lifter to carefully remove jars, without tilting, and place on a towel.

12 Let jars cool, undisturbed, for 12 to 24 hours. Once completely cool, test the seals by gently pressing down on the center of the lids—they should not flex (see page 52).

TIP

For extra flavor, stir in fresh herbs, sour cream, or cooked sausage after reheating.

# CHICKEN SOUP

**YEAR-ROUND | PRESSURE CANNING | YIELD: 7 (32-OZ) QUART OR 14 (16-OZ) PINT JARS**

*This is the soup that grandmothers have been making for generations—a remedy for sniffles, a cure for homesick hearts, and a simple pleasure on a chilly day. Using pasture-raised chicken not only enriches the depth of flavor, but also provides a richer, more nutrient-dense broth, full of collagen and essential minerals.*

### INGREDIENTS

2 quarts chicken stock (page 146), visible fat skimmed if homemade

2 to 3 cups shredded cooked chicken (from a roasted or simmered whole chicken)

3 cups diced carrots

3 cups diced celery

2 cups diced yellow onions

1 cup diced peeled potatoes

1 tsp sea salt (optional)

1 tsp dried thyme

1 tsp dried parsley

½ tsp freshly ground black pepper

### INSTRUCTIONS

1   In a large stockpot, combine stock, shredded chicken, vegetables, salt (if using), thyme, parsley, and pepper. Bring to a gentle boil over medium-high heat, then reduce heat and simmer for 10 to 15 minutes, or until vegetables are slightly softened but still firm. (The vegetables will continue to cook during canning.)

2   Meanwhile, prepare jars, bands, and lids for canning and keep warm (see page 49).

3   Ladle the hot soup into prepared jars, leaving 1-inch headspace. Remove bubbles using a bubble remover (see page 49).

4   Using a clean, damp cloth or paper towel, wipe rims clean. Place sterilized lids on jars. Then screw on bands and tighten just until fingertip-tight (see page 49).

5   Fill your pressure canner with 2 to 3 inches of water. (Check your model's manual for exact recommendations.)

6   Load jars onto rack in pressure canner, ensuring they don't touch. Affix canner lid and turn heat to high.

7   Once canner is steaming, allow it to vent steam for 10 minutes before closing the vent or adding the weight (see page 50).

8   Bring canner to the correct PSI for your model and altitude (see page 199). Process pints for 75 minutes and quarts for 90 minutes. (Start timer only when canner reaches correct pressure.)

9  Turn off heat and allow the canner to cool naturally. Do not remove the lid or regulator until the pressure gauge reads zero. Tilt the lid away from your face when opening the canner.

10  Use jar lifter to carefully remove jars, without tilting, and place on a towel.

11  Let jars cool, undisturbed, for 12 to 24 hours. Once completely cool, test the seals by gently pressing down on the center of the lids—they should not flex (see page 52).

### TIPS

Avoid thickeners: Do not add flour, cornstarch, or dairy before canning. These can interfere with heat penetration and safety.

Ensure fat has been fully skimmed from stock before canning to prevent spoilage.

To enhance flavor, add fresh herbs like dill or parsley when reheating.

### VARIATION

For a creamy chicken soup, stir in ½ cup milk or cream when reheating.

CHAPTER 9

# ONE-JAR MEALS

Pickled Three Bean Salad 170

Pickled Vegetable Medley 172

Chicken and Vegetable Stew 174

Pork and Beans 176

Basic Chili 178

Beef and Root Vegetable Chili 180

Sloppy Joe Filling 182

Meatballs in Sauce 184

Beef Stew 186

## MEAL PLANNING

Preserved meals in jars are the ultimate time-saver, offering convenience without sacrificing quality or flavor. Here are some tips to help you make the most of your homemade canned meals.

## MENU PLANNING

Plan your week with a mix of canned meals and fresh dishes. Use canned chili or soups for busy nights and save time-intensive meals for weekends. Incorporate leftovers creatively, such as using meatballs in sandwiches or serving chili over baked potatoes.

## ROTATE YOUR PANTRY

Incorporate meals in jars into your weekly rotation and ensure you use older jars first. Label jars with the date of canning, and plan menus to prevent waste while keeping meals fresh and flavorful. For example, plan a "pantry week" once a month to focus on using preserved meals.

## THEME NIGHTS

Build your menu around themes to simplify planning. Use meals in jars as a foundation.

**Italian Night:** Serve meatballs in sauce (page 184) over pasta with a side of garlic bread.

**Soup and Salad Night:** Pair mixed bean soup (page 164) with a fresh garden salad.

**Tex-Mex Night:** Heat up chili (page 178) and serve with cornbread, tortilla chips, or baked potatoes.

## BATCH COOKING ADD-ONS

Use canned meals as the base for batch cooking larger meals. For example:

Combine beef stew (see page 186) with fresh vegetables for a pot pie filling.

Use mixed bean soup (page 164) as a starter for a casserole or as a thickener for a hearty stew.

# PICKLED THREE BEAN SALAD

LATE SUMMER | WATER BATH | YIELD: 6 (16-OZ) PINT JARS

*This crisp, tangy, and slightly sweet three-bean salad is a classic. Packed with vibrant colors and bold pickled flavors, it's perfect as a refreshing side dish, a tangy salad topping, or a zesty snack straight from the jar.*

## INGREDIENTS

2 cups chopped green beans
(cut into 2-inch pieces)

2 cups chopped wax beans
(cut into 2-inch pieces)

1 cup cooked or canned kidney beans,
rinsed and drained

1 large red onion, thinly sliced

2 cups pickling vinegar (5% acidity)

1 cup water

1 cup granulated sugar

1 tbsp mustard seeds

1 tsp celery seeds

1 tsp sea salt

## INSTRUCTIONS

1  Fill your water canner roughly three-quarters full of water. Bring to a boil over high heat.

2  Prepare jars, bands, and lids for canning and keep warm (see page 33).

3  Prepare beans: In a large bowl, prepare an ice bath. Bring a large pot of water to a boil. Add beans to water and boil (blanch) for 3 minutes. Using a slotted spoon or spider, transfer blanched beans to the ice bath. Drain well.

4  Make brine: In a medium saucepan, combine vinegar, water, sugar, mustard seeds, celery seeds, and salt. Bring to a boil, stirring until the sugar has completely dissolved.

5  Layer green beans, wax beans, kidney beans, and onion in prepared jars.

6  Ladle the hot brine into jars, ensuring vegetables are fully submerged. Leave ½-inch headspace. Remove bubbles using a bubble remover (see page 34).

7  Using a clean, damp cloth or paper towel, wipe rims clean. Place sterilized lids on jars. Then screw on bands and tighten just until fingertip-tight (see page 34).

8  Using a jar lifter, place jars in canner rack. Submerge rack in boiling water, ensuring jars are covered by at least 1 inch of water. (You may need to add a little extra boiling water.) Cover canner with lid and bring water to a rolling boil.

9  Process jars for 15 minutes (adjust for altitude, if needed; see page 198). At end of processing time, turn off heat and remove lid.

10  Once water has stopped boiling, use jar lifter to carefully remove jars, without tilting, and place on a towel.

11  Let jars cool, undisturbed, for 12 to 24 hours. Once completely cool, test the seals by gently pressing down on the center of the lids—they should not flex (see page 35).

# PICKLED VEGETABLE MEDLEY

LATE SUMMER | WATER BATH | YIELD: 6 (16-OZ) PINT JARS

*A bright, tangy vegetable mix that's perfect for antipasto platters, sandwiches, salads, or as a flavorful side dish. Mix with pasta and feta for a quick Mediterranean dish. The brine preserves freshness while enhancing the natural crunch of the vegetables. Set aside for 2 weeks before enjoying to let the flavors meld.*

## INGREDIENTS

2 cups cauliflower florets

2 cups chopped green beans (cut into 2-inch pieces)

2 cups carrot slices

1 cup red bell pepper strips

1 cup yellow bell pepper strips

1 large red onion, thinly sliced

2 cups pickling vinegar (5% acidity)

1 cup water

½ cup olive oil

¼ cup granulated sugar

1 tbsp mustard seeds

1 tsp dried oregano

1 tsp sea salt

½ tsp crushed red pepper flakes (optional)

## INSTRUCTIONS

1   Fill your water bath canner halfway up the pot. Bring to a simmer.

2   Prepare jars, bands, and lids for canning and keep warm (see page 33).

3   Prepare vegetables: In a large bowl, prepare an ice bath. Bring a large pot of water to a boil. Working in separate batches, boil (blanch) cauliflower, green beans, and carrots for 3 minutes each. Using a slotted spoon or spider, transfer blanched vegetables to the ice bath. Drain well.

4   Make brine: In a medium saucepan, combine vinegar, water, olive oil, sugar, mustard seeds, oregano, salt, and red pepper flakes (if using). Bring to a boil, stirring until the sugar has completely dissolved.

5   Layer cauliflower, green beans, carrots, bell peppers, and red onion slices in prepared jars. Pack vegetables tightly but allow space for the brine to flow.

6   Ladle the hot brine into jars, ensuring the vegetables are fully submerged. Leave ½-inch headspace. Remove bubbles using a bubble remover (see page 34).

7   Using a clean, damp cloth or paper towel, wipe rims clean. Place sterilized lids on jars. Then screw on bands and tighten just until fingertip-tight (see page 34).

8   Using a jar lifter, place jars in canner rack. Submerge rack in boiling water, ensuring jars are covered by at least 1 inch of water. (You may need to add a little extra boiling water.) Cover canner with lid and bring water to a rolling boil.

9   Process jars for 15 minutes (adjust for altitude, if needed; see page 198). At end of processing time, turn off heat and remove lid.

10  Once water has stopped boiling, use jar lifter to carefully remove jars, without tilting, and place on a towel.

11  Let jars cool, undisturbed, for 12 to 24 hours. Once completely cool, test the seals by gently pressing down on the center of the lids—they should not flex (see page 35).

# CHICKEN AND VEGETABLE STEW

YEAR-ROUND | PRESSURE CANNING | YIELD: 6 (32-OZ) QUART JARS

*This hearty, all-in-one meal combines tender chicken, nutrient-rich vegetables, and a flavorful stock for a quick and convenient meal straight from the jar. Serve it over rice, egg noodles, or with crusty bread for a comforting, protein-packed dinner any time of year.*

## INGREDIENTS

6 cups chicken stock (page 146), visible fat skimmed if homemade (or low-sodium if store-bought)

4 pounds boneless chicken thighs or breasts, cut into 1-inch cubes

3 cups diced carrots

3 cups diced celery

3 cups diced peeled potatoes

1 large yellow onion, diced

1½ tsp dried thyme, divided

1½ tsp dried parsley, divided

1½ tsp freshly ground black pepper, divided

3 tsp sea salt, divided

6 bay leaves, divided

## INSTRUCTIONS

1  Prepare jars, bands, and lids for canning and keep warm (see page 49).

2  Heat stock in a stockpot over medium heat until warm.

3  Evenly distribute the chicken, carrots, celery, potatoes, and onions in prepared jars, leaving 1-inch headspace. Do not overpack.

4  To each prepared jar, add ¼ tsp each thyme, parsley, and black pepper, along with ½ tsp salt and 1 bay leaf.

5  Ladle the hot stock into jars, maintaining 1-inch headspace. Remove bubbles using a bubble remover (see page 49).

6  Using a clean, damp cloth or paper towel, wipe rims clean. Place sterilized lids on jars. Then screw on bands and tighten just until fingertip-tight (see page 49).

7  Fill your pressure canner with 2 to 3 inches of water. (Check your model's manual for exact recommendations.)

8  Load jars onto rack in pressure canner, ensuring they don't touch. Affix canner lid and turn heat to high.

9  Once canner is steaming, allow it to vent steam for 10 minutes before closing the vent or adding the weight (see page 50).

10  Bring canner to the correct PSI for your model and altitude (see page 199). Process jars for 75 minutes. (Start timer only when the canner reaches the correct pressure.)

11  Turn off heat and allow the canner to cool naturally. Do not remove the lid or regulator until the pressure gauge reads zero. Tilt the lid away from your face when opening the canner.

12  Use jar lifter to carefully remove jars, without tilting, and place on a towel.

13  Let jars cool, undisturbed, for 12 to 24 hours. Once completely cool, test the seals by gently pressing down on the center of the lids—they should not flex (see page 52).

---

TIP

To reheat, pour stew into a saucepan over medium heat, stirring occasionally until warmed through.

---

VARIATIONS

**Make it creamy:** When reheating, stir in ¼ cup heavy cream, coconut milk, or sour cream.

**Thicken the broth:** When reheating, whisk together 1 tbsp cornstarch and 2 tbsp water, then add to broth and continue to heat, stirring, until thickened.

**Add extra vegetables:** Stir in 1 cup diced zucchini or chopped green beans during reheating.

**Add depth:** In Step 4, add ¼ tsp smoked paprika per jar for a subtly smoky, savory flavor.

# PORK AND BEANS

**YEAR-ROUND | PRESSURE CANNING | YIELD: 6 (16-OZ) PINT JARS**

*Pork and beans is a classic comfort food, combining tender navy beans, smoky pork, and a tangy, slightly sweet tomato sauce. This hearty, protein-packed dish makes for a quick and satisfying meal, perfect for pairing with cornbread, baked potatoes, or serving over rice.*

### INGREDIENTS

½ cup diced bacon or salt pork, trimmed of visible fat

6 cups tomato sauce (homemade or low-sodium if store-bought)

¼ cup molasses

2 tbsp apple cider vinegar (5% acidity)

1 tsp Worcestershire sauce

1 tsp smoked paprika

1 tsp mustard powder

1 tsp sea salt

½ tsp chili powder

4 cups cooked or canned navy beans, rinsed and drained

### INSTRUCTIONS

1   Prepare jars, bands, and lids for canning and keep warm (see page 49).

2   Cook pork: In a large skillet over medium heat, cook diced bacon or salt pork until lightly crisped. Drain excess fat and set aside.

3   In a large stockpot, combine tomato sauce, molasses, apple cider vinegar, Worcestershire sauce, smoked paprika, mustard powder, salt, and chili powder. Stir well.

4   Add cooked navy beans and browned pork to the sauce. Bring to a gentle boil, then reduce heat and simmer for 5 to 10 minutes, allowing flavors to meld.

5   Ladle the pork and beans into prepared jars, leaving 1-inch headspace. Remove bubbles using a bubble remover (see page 49).

6   Using a clean, damp cloth or paper towel, wipe rims clean. Place sterilized lids on jars. Then screw on bands and tighten just until fingertip-tight (see page 49).

7   Fill your pressure canner with 2 to 3 inches of water. (Check your model's manual for exact recommendations.)

8   Load jars onto rack in pressure canner, ensuring they don't touch. Affix canner lid and turn heat to high.

9   Once canner is steaming, allow it to vent steam for 10 minutes before closing the vent or adding the weight (see page 50).

10  Bring canner to the correct PSI for your model and altitude (see page 199). Process jars for 75 minutes. (Start timer only when the canner reaches the correct pressure.)

11  Turn off heat and allow the canner to cool naturally. Do not remove the lid or regulator until the pressure gauge reads zero. Tilt the lid away from your face when opening the canner.

12  Use jar lifter to carefully remove jars, without tilting, and place on a towel.

13  Let jars cool, undisturbed, for 12 to 24 hours. Once completely cool, test the seals by gently pressing down on the center of the lids—they should not flex (see page 52).

## TIPS

Trim excess pork fat before cooking to prevent spoilage.

Avoid adding flour or cornstarch before canning, as thickening agents can interfere with safe processing.

## VARIATIONS

**Sweet and Smoky Beans:** Add 1 extra tbsp molasses for a richer, sweeter flavor.

**Spicy Pork and Beans:** Increase chili powder to 1 tsp for a bolder, spicier kick.

**Vegetarian Beans:** Omit pork and add ½ tsp liquid smoke for a meat-free version.

# BASIC CHILI

**YEAR-ROUND | PRESSURE CANNING | YIELD: 6 (32-OZ) QUART OR 12 (16-OZ) PINT JARS**

*This deeply flavorful chili is perfect for quick meals, camping trips, or hearty weeknight dinners. Just reheat and serve over rice, cornbread, or baked potatoes for a comforting, protein-packed meal.*

### INGREDIENTS

4 pounds 80/20 ground beef (preferably grass-fed, grass-finished, and pasture-raised)

2 large yellow onions, diced

4 cloves garlic, minced

8 cups crushed tomatoes

4 cups cooked or canned kidney beans or black beans, rinsed and drained

2 cups beef stock (page 148), visible fat skimmed if homemade, or water

¼ cup chili powder

2 tsp ground cumin

1 tsp smoked paprika

2 tsp sea salt

½ tsp freshly ground black pepper

½ tsp crushed red pepper flakes (optional)

### INSTRUCTIONS

1 Prepare jars, bands, and lids for canning and keep warm (see page 49).

2 In a large skillet over medium-high heat, cook ground beef until browned. Drain excess fat and set aside.

3 In the same skillet, sauté onions and garlic for 5 minutes until softened.

4 In a large stockpot, combine browned beef, sautéed onions, garlic, crushed tomatoes, beans, stock, and seasonings (if using). Bring to a boil, then reduce heat and simmer for 10 minutes.

5 Ladle the hot chili into prepared jars, leaving 1-inch headspace. Remove bubbles using a bubble remover (see page 49).

6 Using a clean, damp cloth or paper towel, wipe rims clean. Place sterilized lids on jars. Then screw on bands and tighten just until fingertip-tight (see page 49).

7 Fill your pressure canner with 2 to 3 inches of water. (Check your model's manual for exact recommendations.)

8 Load jars onto rack in pressure canner, ensuring they don't touch. Affix canner lid and turn heat to high.

9 Once canner is steaming, allow it to vent steam for 10 minutes before closing the vent or adding the weight (see page 50).

10  Bring canner to the correct PSI for your model and altitude (see page 199). Process pints for 75 minutes or quarts for 90 minutes. (Start timer only when the canner reaches the correct pressure.)

11  Turn off heat and allow the canner to cool naturally. Do not remove the lid or regulator until the pressure gauge reads zero. Tilt the lid away from your face when opening the canner.

12  Use jar lifter to carefully remove jars, without tilting, and place on a towel.

13  Let jars cool, undisturbed, for 12 to 24 hours. Once completely cool, test the seals by gently pressing down on the center of the lids—they should not flex (see page 52).

---

## TIPS

For thicker chili: Stir in 2 tbsp tomato paste after reheating.

Do not add dairy, flour, or thickeners before canning, as they can interfere with safe processing.

---

## VARIATIONS

**Turkey Chili:** Substitute 4 pounds ground turkey for the beef, use black beans instead of kidney beans, and replace the beef stock with chicken stock.

**Spicy Chili:** Increase quantity of red pepper flakes to 1 tsp or add 1 finely diced jalapeño.

**Smoky and Sweet Chili:** In Step 4, stir in 1 tbsp pure maple syrup and ½ tsp chipotle powder.

# BEEF AND ROOT VEGETABLE CHILI

## WINTER | PRESSURE CANNING | YIELD: 6 (32-OZ) QUART JARS

*Inspired by Emeril Lagasse's bold flavors, this is a hearty, rich chili packed with ground beef, root vegetables, and bold spices. Serve over rice or cornbread and garnish with sour cream, shredded cheddar, and/or fresh cilantro.*

### INGREDIENTS

4 pounds ground beef

1 large yellow onion, diced

2 cups diced carrots

1 cup diced parsnips (or substitute sweet potatoes)

6 cups cooked or canned kidney beans, rinsed and drained

6 cups crushed tomatoes

2 cups beef stock (page 148), visible fat skimmed if homemade

¼ cup chili powder

2 tsp ground cumin

1 tsp smoked paprika

1 tsp dried oregano

2 tsp sea salt

½ tsp freshly ground black pepper

### INSTRUCTIONS

1   Prepare jars, bands, and lids for canning and keep warm (see page 49).

2   In a large skillet over medium-high heat, cook ground beef until browned. Drain and discard excess fat. Set side.

3   In the same skillet, sauté onions, carrots, and parsnips for 5 minutes, or until softened.

4   In a large stockpot, combine browned beef, sautéed vegetables, beans, tomatoes, stock, and seasonings. Bring to a boil, then reduce heat and simmer for 10 minutes.

5   Ladle the hot chili into prepared jars, leaving 1-inch headspace. Remove bubbles using a bubble remover (see page 49).

6   Using a clean, damp cloth or paper towel, wipe rims clean. Place sterilized lids on jars. Then screw on bands and tighten just until fingertip-tight (see page 49).

7   Fill your pressure canner with 2 to 3 inches of water. (Check your model's manual for exact recommendations.)

8   Load jars onto rack in pressure canner, ensuring they don't touch. Affix canner lid and turn heat to high.

9   Once canner is steaming, allow it to vent steam for 10 minutes before closing the vent or adding the weight (see page 50).

10 Bring canner to the correct PSI for your model and altitude (see page 199). Process jars for 90 minutes. (Start timer only when the canner reaches the correct pressure.)

11 Turn off heat and allow the canner to cool naturally. Do not remove the lid or regulator until the pressure gauge reads zero. Tilt the lid away from your face when opening the canner.

12 Use a jar lifter to carefully remove jars, without tilting, and place on a towel.

13 Let jars cool, undisturbed, for 12 to 24 hours. Once completely cool, test the seals by gently pressing down on the center of the lids—they should not flex (see page 52).

## TIPS

For thicker chili: Stir in 2 tbsp tomato paste per serving after reheating.

Do not add dairy, flour, or thickeners before canning, as they can interfere with safe processing.

## VARIATIONS

**Spicy Chili:** In Step 3, add 1 finely diced jalapeño.

**Rich and Deep Flavor:** In Step 4, stir in ½ tsp unsweetened cocoa powder.

**Leaner Option:** Substitute an equal amount of ground turkey for the beef, and use chicken stock instead of beef stock.

# SLOPPY JOE FILLING
## YEAR-ROUND | PRESSURE CANNING | YIELD: 7 (16-OZ) PINT JARS

*A rich, savory Sloppy Joe filling made with ground beef, tangy tomato sauce, and a touch of sweetness. Perfect for quick weeknight meals. Try it as a taco filling. Or serve on toasted buns or over baked potatoes for a hearty meal.*

### INGREDIENTS

4 pounds ground beef

1 large yellow onion, finely diced

1 green bell pepper, finely diced

2 cups tomato sauce

½ cup tomato paste

¼ cup apple cider vinegar (5% acidity)

3 tbsp molasses or liquid honey

1 tbsp Worcestershire sauce (optional)

2 tsp sea salt

1 tsp mustard powder

1 tsp smoked paprika

½ tsp garlic powder

¼ tsp cayenne pepper (optional)

### INSTRUCTIONS

1   Prepare jars, bands, and lids for canning and keep warm (see page 49).

2   In a large skillet over medium-high heat, cook ground beef in batches until browned. Drain excess fat and set aside.

3   In the same skillet, sauté onion and pepper for 3 to 4 minutes, or until translucent.

4   In a large stockpot, combine tomato sauce, tomato paste, apple cider vinegar, molasses, Worcestershire sauce (if using), and spices (if using). Stir in browned beef and sautéed vegetables. Bring to a boil, then reduce heat and simmer for 10 minutes.

5   Ladle the hot sloppy joe filling into prepared jars, leaving 1-inch headspace. Remove bubbles using a bubble remover (see page 49).

6   Using a clean, damp cloth or paper towel, wipe rims clean. Place sterilized lids on jars. Then screw on bands and tighten just until fingertip-tight (see page 49).

7   Fill your pressure canner with 2 to 3 inches of water. (Check your model's manual for exact recommendations.)

8   Load jars onto rack in pressure canner, ensuring they don't touch. Affix canner lid and turn heat to high.

9   Once canner is steaming, allow it to vent steam for 10 minutes before closing the vent or adding the weight (see page 50).

10  Bring canner to the correct PSI for your model and altitude (see page 199). Process jars for 75 minutes. (Start timer only when the canner reaches the correct pressure.)

11  Turn off heat and allow the canner to cool naturally. Do not remove the lid or regulator until the pressure gauge reads zero. Tilt the lid away from your face when opening the canner.

12  Use a jar lifter to carefully remove jars, without tilting, and place on a towel.

13  Let jars cool, undisturbed, for 12 to 24 hours. Once completely cool, test the seals by gently pressing down on the center of the lids—they should not flex (see page 52).

---

TIP

For a leaner option, substitute ground turkey for the beef.

# MEATBALLS IN SAUCE

YEAR-ROUND | PRESSURE CANNING | YIELD: 6 (32-OZ) QUART JARS

*These tender meatballs simmered in a rich tomato sauce make a perfect pantry staple for quick, hearty meals. Serve over pasta or zucchini noodles, topped with Parmesan and fresh basil. Or use it to make meatball subs!*

## INGREDIENTS

### For the Meatballs:

3 pounds ground beef or a mix of ground beef and pork

¼ cup finely chopped fresh parsley, leaves and stems

1 tsp garlic powder

1 tsp onion powder

1 tsp sea salt

½ tsp freshly ground black pepper

1 tbsp olive oil

### For the Sauce:

8 cups crushed tomatoes (pourable consistency)

1 large yellow onion, diced

3 cloves garlic, minced

2 tsp dried basil

1 tsp dried oregano

1 tsp sea salt

½ tsp smoked paprika

½ tsp freshly ground black pepper

1 cup beef stock (to thin sauce, plus more as needed), visible fat skimmed if homemade

## INSTRUCTIONS

1 Prepare jars, bands, and lids for canning and keep warm (see page 49).

2 Make meatballs: In a large bowl, gently combine ground meat, parsley, garlic powder, onion powder, salt, and pepper just until incorporated. Avoid overmixing to maintain tenderness. Using your hands, form the mixture into 1-inch meatballs, handling gently to preserve texture.

3 In a large skillet over medium heat, add 1 tbsp olive oil and lightly brown meatballs on all sides, turning occasionally. (Do not fully cook—this ensures safe canning and prevents toughness.)

4 Make sauce: In a large stockpot, combine tomatoes, onion, garlic, stock, basil, oregano, salt, smoked paprika, and black pepper. Cook over medium-high heat for 10 minutes, stirring occasionally. (Ensure the sauce is pourable; add stock if needed.)

5 Place 8 to 10 meatballs in each prepared jar.

6 Ladle the hot tomato sauce over the meatballs, leaving 1-inch headspace. Remove bubbles using a bubble remover (see page 49).

7   Using a clean, damp cloth or paper towel, wipe rims clean. Place sterilized lids on jars. Then screw on bands and tighten just until fingertip-tight (see page 49).

8   Fill your pressure canner with 2 to 3 inches of water. (Check your model's manual for exact recommendations.)

9   Load jars onto rack in pressure canner, ensuring they don't touch. Affix canner lid and turn heat to high.

10  Once canner is steaming, allow it to vent steam for 10 minutes before closing the vent or adding the weight (see page 50).

11  Bring canner to the correct PSI for your model and altitude (see page 199). Process jars for 90 minutes. (Start timer only when the canner reaches the correct pressure.)

12  Turn off heat and allow the canner to cool naturally. Do not remove the lid or regulator until the pressure gauge reads zero. Tilt the lid away from your face when opening the canner.

13  Use a jar lifter to carefully remove jars, without tilting, and place on a towel.

14  Let jars cool, undisturbed, for 12 to 24 hours. Once completely cool, test the seals by gently pressing down on the center of the lids—they should not flex (see page 52).

TIPS

Follow safe canning practices and avoid adding breadcrumbs or eggs to the meatballs.

Sauce must be thin enough (pourable) to allow proper canning.

# BEEF STEW

YEAR-ROUND | PRESSURE CANNING | YIELD: 7 (32-OZ) QUART JARS

*This hearty beef stew is packed with tender chunks of beef, fresh vegetables, and savory stock. Serve over mashed potatoes or with crusty bread for a complete meal.*

## INGREDIENTS

3 pounds beef chuck or stew meat, trimmed of excess fat and cut into 1-inch cubes

2 quarts beef stock (page 148), visible fat skimmed if homemade

3 cups diced carrots

3 cups diced celery

3 cups diced potatoes

2 cups diced onions

1 tsp sea salt (optional)

1 tsp dried thyme

1 tsp dried rosemary

½ tsp freshly ground black pepper

## INSTRUCTIONS

1  Prepare jars, bands, and lids for canning and keep warm (see page 49).

2  Brown beef (optional, but recommended for depth of flavor): In a large skillet over medium-high heat, cook beef in batches until browned. (Be careful not to overcrowd the pan.) Remove pan from heat and set aside.

3  In a large stockpot, combine stock, browned beef, carrots, celery, potatoes, onions, salt (if using), thyme, rosemary, and black pepper. Bring the mixture to a gentle boil over medium-high heat, then reduce heat and simmer for 5 minutes to allow flavors to meld.

4  Ladle the hot stew into prepared jars: Distribute the solids evenly among the jars and then cover with the stock, maintaining 1-inch headspace. Remove bubbles using a bubble remover (see page 49).

5  Using a clean, damp cloth or paper towel, wipe rims clean. Place sterilized lids on jars. Then screw on bands and tighten just until fingertip-tight (see page 49).

6  Fill your pressure canner with 2 to 3 inches of water. (Check your model's manual for exact recommendations.)

7  Load jars onto rack in pressure canner, ensuring they don't touch. Affix canner lid and turn heat to high.

8  Once canner is steaming, allow it to vent steam for 10 minutes before closing the vent or adding the weight (see page 50).

9   Bring canner to the correct PSI for your model and altitude (see page 199). Process jars for 90 minutes. (Start timer only when the canner reaches the correct pressure.)

10   Turn off heat and allow the canner to cool naturally. Do not remove the lid or regulator until the pressure gauge reads zero. Tilt the lid away from your face when opening the canner.

11   Use jar lifter to carefully remove jars, without tilting, and place on a towel.

12   Let jars cool, undisturbed, for 12 to 24 hours. Once completely cool, test the seals by gently pressing down on the center of the lids—they should not flex (see page 52).

## TIPS

For a thicker stew: After reheating, stir in a flour or cornstarch slurry (1 tbsp flour or cornstarch mixed with 2 tbsp water per jar) and simmer until thickened.

For extra flavor: In Step 3, add ½ cup dry red wine, before simmering.

CHAPTER 10

# DESSERTS
# IN JARS

Berry Syrup               190          Apple Pie Filling        193

Fruit Compote             191          Cherry Pie Filling       194

Pudding Topping           192          Peach Pie Filling        196

## SWEET SUCCESS

Perfecting dessert preserves means balancing timing, technique, and creativity to capture seasonal flavors year-round. From achieving the perfect set to adjusting sugar ratios, the following tips will help you elevate your sweet creations.

## ACHIEVING THE PERFECT SET

Testing gel points is essential for dessert preserves. Keep a chilled plate in your freezer while cooking. When ready, drop a spoonful onto the plate and run your finger through it. If the mixture wrinkles and holds its shape, it's done. If the mixture fails the gel test (i.e., it runs instead of wrinkling and holding its shape), continue cooking and test again every 2 to 3 minutes. Stir frequently to prevent scorching and check for signs of thickening. Depending on the fruit's natural pectin content and moisture levels, it may take 5 to 15 additional minutes to reach the correct gel stage.

For even more accuracy, use a candy thermometer—the gel point for jam is typically around 220°F at sea level (adjust for altitude as needed).

This simple test is more reliable than timers.

## REFINING SUGAR RATIOS

Sugar ensures proper setting and preservation. While a 1:1 fruit-to-sugar ratio provides consistency, you can safely reduce the sugar in dessert preserves by up to one-third by adding natural pectin sources like grated green apple or citrus peel.

For every 1 cup of reduced sugar, add:

- 2 tbsp grated green apple (high in natural pectin)
- 1 tbsp finely chopped citrus peel (lemon or orange work best)
- 1 tbsp bottled lemon juice (to maintain acidity for safe preservation)

## SERVING IDEAS

For elegant desserts, pair tart jams with cheeses, drizzle syrups over cakes, or glaze pastries with spiced preserves.

# BERRY SYRUP
## SUMMER | WATER BATH | YIELD: 6 (16-OZ) PINT JARS

*Sweet and versatile, this berry syrup is the ultimate summer condiment. Whether drizzled over pancakes, ice cream, or baked goods, it brings vibrant fruit flavors to every dish.*

## INGREDIENTS

6 cups mixed berries (e.g., blueberries, rasp-berries, and strawberries), hulled if needed

4 cups granulated sugar

2 cups water

2 tbsp bottled lemon juice

## INSTRUCTIONS

1 Fill your water canner roughly three-quarters full of water. Bring to a boil over high heat.

2 Prepare jars, bands, and lids for canning and keep warm (see page 33).

3 In a large, deep saucepan, combine berries, sugar, and water. Cook over medium heat for 10 to 15 minutes, stirring occasionally, until the berries break down and release their juices.

4 Strain the cooked berries through a fine-mesh sieve or cheesecloth into a clean saucepan. Press gently using the back of a spoon to extract as much liquid as possible. Discard the solids or save them for another use.

5 Stir in lemon juice, then bring the mixture to a gentle boil.

6 Ladle the hot syrup into prepared jars, leaving ¼-inch headspace. Remove bubbles using a bubble remover (see page 34).

7 Using a clean, damp cloth or paper towel, wipe rims clean. Place sterilized lids on jars. Then screw on bands and tighten just until fingertip-tight (see page 34).

8 Using a jar lifter, place jars in the canner rack. Submerge the rack in boiling water, ensuring jars are covered by at least 1 inch of water. (You may need to add a little extra boiling water.) Cover canner with the lid and bring water to a rolling boil.

9 Process jars for 10 minutes (adjust for altitude, if needed; see page 198). At end of processing time, turn off heat and remove lid.

10 Once water has stopped boiling, use a jar lifter to carefully remove jars, without tilting, and place on a towel.

11 Let jars cool, undisturbed, for 12 to 24 hours. Once completely cool, test the seals by gently pressing down on the center of the lids—they should not flex (see page 35).

# FRUIT COMPOTE

YEAR-ROUND | WATER BATH | YIELD: 6 (16-OZ) PINT JARS

*This versatile fruit compote blends apples, pears, and plums for a perfect balance of sweetness and tartness. Use it as a topping for cheesecake, yogurt, or waffles.*

## INGREDIENTS

6 cups chopped mixed fruits
(e.g., apples, pears, and pitted plums)

3 cups granulated sugar

2 cups water

1 tsp pure vanilla extract

1 tsp ground cinnamon (optional)

## INSTRUCTIONS

1 Fill your water canner roughly three-quarters full of water. Bring to a boil over high heat.

2 Prepare jars, bands, and lids for canning and keep warm (see page 33).

3 In a large, deep saucepan, combine mixed fruits, sugar, and water. Cook over medium heat until the fruit has softened but still hold its shape, about 10 minutes.

4 Stir in vanilla and cinnamon (if using). Simmer for 5 more minutes.

5 Ladle the hot compote into prepared jars, leaving ½-inch headspace. Remove bubbles using a bubble remover (see page 34).

6 Using a clean, damp cloth or paper towel, wipe rims clean. Place sterilized lids on jars. Then screw on bands and tighten just until fingertip-tight (see page 34).

7 Using a jar lifter, place jars in canner rack. Submerge rack in boiling water, ensuring jars are covered by at least 1 inch of water. (You may need to add a little extra boiling water.) Cover canner with lid and bring water to a rolling boil.

8 Process jars for 20 minutes (adjust for altitude, if needed; see page 198). At end of processing time, turn off heat and remove lid.

9 Once water has stopped boiling, use jar lifter to carefully remove jars, without tilting, and place on a towel.

10 Let jars cool, undisturbed, for 12 to 24 hours. Once completely cool, test the seals by gently pressing down on the center of the lids—they should not flex (see page 35).

# MARMALADE PUDDING TOPPING

WINTER | WATER BATH | YIELD: 5 (16-OZ) PINT JARS

*This marmalade pudding topping takes everything you love about traditional marmalade—its zesty citrus flavor and vibrant color—and transforms it into a silky, spoonable topping perfect for drizzling over pound cakes, scones, and breakfast pastries. Swirl into yogurt or oatmeal for a burst of citrus flavor. Glaze roasted fruits or cheesecakes to add a glossy, flavorful finish.*

## INGREDIENTS

4 cups peeled, seeded, and finely chopped citrus fruits (e.g., oranges and lemons)

4 cups granulated sugar

1 cup water

1 tbsp finely grated fresh ginger (optional)

## INSTRUCTIONS

1   Fill your water canner roughly three-quarters full of water. Bring to a boil over high heat.

2   Prepare jars, bands, and lids for canning and keep warm (see page 33).

3   In a large, deep saucepan, combine chopped fruit, sugar, and water. Cook over medium heat until thickened to a jam-like consistency, 20 to 30 minutes.

4   Stir in ginger (if using). Simmer for 5 more minutes.

5   Ladle the hot marmalade into prepared jars, leaving ¼-inch headspace. Remove bubbles using a bubble remover (see page 34).

6   Using a clean, damp cloth or paper towel, wipe rims clean. Place sterilized lids on jars. Then screw on bands and tighten just until fingertip-tight (see page 34).

7   Using a jar lifter, place jars in canner rack. Submerge rack in boiling water, ensuring jars are covered by at least 1 inch of water. (You may need to add a little extra boiling water.) Cover canner with lid and bring water to a rolling boil.

8   Process jars for 15 minutes (adjust for altitude, if needed; see page 198). At end of processing time, turn off heat and remove lid.

9   Once water has stopped boiling, use jar lifter to carefully remove jars, without tilting, and place on a towel.

10   Let jars cool, undisturbed, for 12 to 24 hours. Once completely cool, test the seals by gently pressing down on the center of the lids—they should not flex (see page 35).

# PEACH PIE FILLING

## SUMMER | WATER BATH | YIELD: 5 (32-OZ) QUART JARS

*Capture the taste of summer with this sweet, tangy peach pie filling. Gently spiced with cinnamon, it's perfect for pies, cobblers (see page 195), or any dessert needing a hint of sunshine.*

### INGREDIENTS

1½ cups granulated sugar

¼ cup Clear Jel

½ tsp ground cinnamon

2 cups unsweetened peach juice

¾ cup bottled lemon juice

6 cups peaches, peeled, pitted, and sliced

### INSTRUCTIONS

1   Fill your water canner roughly three-quarters full of water. Bring to a boil over high heat.

2   Prepare jars, bands, and lids for canning and keep warm (see page 33).

3   In a large, deep saucepan, whisk together sugar, Clear Jel, and cinnamon. Stir in peach juice. Cook over medium heat, stirring constantly, until the mixture thickens to a smooth, glossy, pudding-like consistency that coats the back of a spoon but remains pourable, 5 to 7 minutes.

4   Stir in lemon juice and sliced peaches. Bring to a boil and simmer for 3 minutes.

5   Ladle the hot peach mixture into prepared jars, leaving 1-inch headspace. Remove bubbles using a bubble remover (see page 34).

6   Using a clean, damp cloth or paper towel, wipe rims clean. Place sterilized lids on jars. Then screw on bands and tighten just until fingertip-tight (see page 34).

7   Using a jar lifter, place jars in canner rack. Submerge rack in boiling water, ensuring jars are covered by at least 1 inch of water. (You may need to add a little extra boiling water.) Cover canner with lid and bring water to a rolling boil.

8   Process jars for 30 minutes (adjust for altitude, if needed; see page 198). At end of processing time, turn off heat and remove lid.

9   Once water has stopped boiling, use jar lifter to carefully remove jars, without tilting, and place on a towel.

10  Let jars cool, undisturbed, for 12 to 24 hours. Once completely cool, test the seals by gently pressing down on the center of the lids—they should not flex (see page 35).

# APPLE PIE FILLING

FALL | WATER BATH | YIELD: 7 (32-OZ) QUART JARS

*With tart apples, warming spices, and a rich syrup, this luscious apple pie filling captures the comforting flavors of autumn.*

## INGREDIENTS

4½ cups granulated sugar

1 cup Clear Jel

1 tbsp ground cinnamon

¼ tsp ground nutmeg

2½ cups unsweetened apple juice

1¼ cups cold water

1 cup bottled lemon juice

6 pounds tart apples, peeled, cored, and sliced

## INSTRUCTIONS

1   Fill your water canner roughly three-quarters full of water. Bring to a boil over high heat.

2   Prepare jars, bands, and lids for canning and keep warm (see page 33).

3   In a large, deep saucepan, whisk together sugar, Clear Jel, cinnamon, and nutmeg. Stir in apple juice and water. Cook over medium heat, stirring constantly, until the mixture reaches a smooth, pourable, yet slightly gel-like consistency, similar to pie filling or a thick gravy, 5 to 10 minutes. It should coat the back of a spoon but still be pourable.

4   Stir in lemon juice and boil for 1 minute.

5   Pack sliced apples tightly into prepared jars, leaving 1-inch headspace.

6   Ladle the hot syrup into jars, maintaining 1-inch headspace. Remove bubbles using a bubble remover (see page 34).

7   Using a clean, damp cloth or paper towel, wipe rims clean. Place sterilized lids on jars. Then screw on bands and tighten just until fingertip-tight (see page 34).

8   Using a jar lifter, place jars in canner rack. Submerge rack in boiling water, ensuring jars are covered by at least 1 inch of water. (You may need to add a little extra boiling water.) Cover canner with lid and bring water to a rolling boil.

9   Process jars for 25 minutes (adjust for altitude, if needed; see page 198). At end of processing time, turn off heat and remove lid.

10  Once water has stopped boiling, use jar lifter to carefully remove jars, without tilting, and place on a towel.

11  Let jars cool, undisturbed, for 12 to 24 hours.
Once completely cool, test the seals by gently
pressing down on the center of the lids—they
should not flex (see page 35).

## MAKE A PIE

1  Pour your prepared filling into a pastry-lined pie
dish, cover with a top crust, and bake at 375°F for
45 to 50 minutes until golden brown.

## MAKE A COBBLER

1  Pour filling into a greased baking dish, top with
biscuit dough, and bake at 375°F for 35 minutes,
until golden brown.

# CHERRY PIE FILLING

SUMMER | WATER BATH | YIELD: 5 (32-OZ) QUART JARS

*Nothing captures the taste of summer quite like homemade cherry pie filling. Whether spooned into a flaky crust for a classic cherry pie, swirled into yogurt, or used as a vibrant topping for waffles and cheesecakes, this filling delivers the perfect balance of tart and sweet.*

## INGREDIENTS

1½ cups granulated sugar

¼ cup Clear Jel

1 cup cold water

1 cup bottled lemon juice

1 tsp pure almond extract (optional)

6 cups pitted cherries

## INSTRUCTIONS

1   Fill your water canner roughly three-quarters full of water. Bring to a boil over high heat.

2   Prepare jars, bands, and lids for canning and keep warm (see page 33).

3   In a large, deep saucepan, whisk together sugar and Clear Jel. Whisk in cold water and cook over medium heat, stirring constantly, until the mixture reaches a smooth, pudding-like consistency that coats the back of a spoon but remains pourable, 5 to 7 minutes.

4   Stir in lemon juice and almond extract (if using). Bring to a boil and simmer for 3 minutes. Gently fold in cherries and simmer for another 3 minutes to allow flavors to meld.

5   Ladle the hot cherry filling into prepared jars, leaving 1-inch headspace. Remove bubbles using a bubble remover.

6   Using a clean, damp cloth or paper towel, wipe rims clean. Place sterilized lids on jars. Then screw on bands and tighten just until fingertip-tight (see page 34).

7   Using a jar lifter, place jars in canner rack. Submerge rack in boiling water, ensuring jars are covered by at least 1 inch of water. (You may need to add a little extra boiling water.) Cover canner with lid and bring water to a rolling boil.

8   Process jars for 30 minutes (adjust for altitude, if needed; see page 198). At end of processing time, turn off heat and remove lid.

9   Once water has stopped boiling, use jar lifter to carefully remove jars, without tilting, and place on a towel.

10  Let jars cool, undisturbed, for 12 to 24 hours. Once completely cool, test the seals by gently pressing down on the center of the lids—they should not flex (see page 35).

## MAKE A PIE

1   For a classic cherry pie, fill a pastry-lined pie dish with your homemade cherry filling. Cover with a lattice crust, brush with egg wash, and bake at 400°F for 45 to 50 minutes, until golden brown and bubbling. Serve warm with a scoop of vanilla ice cream for the ultimate summer dessert!

# REFERENCE CHARTS

When it comes to canning, temperature is the key to preserving food safely and keeping your pantry stocked with confidence. Whether you're using a water bath for high-acid foods or pressure canning low-acid ingredients, hitting the right temperature ensures that harmful bacteria are destroyed and that your jars remain safe for long-term storage.

## WATER BATH CANNING

The water in your water bath canning pot must remain at a rolling boil (212°F) throughout the processing time to ensure proper sterilization. Note that you must account for your location's altitude, as it affects water's boiling point and pressure levels.

**Rule:** Add 5 minutes to the processing time for every 1,000 feet above sea level.

| FOOD TYPE | JAR SIZE | PROCESSING TIME (MINUTES) | ALTITUDE ADJUSTMENTS (+ MINUTES) | TEMPERATURE |
|---|---|---|---|---|
| Jams and jellies | Half-Pint/Pint | 10 | + 5 (1,000 to 6,000 ft), + 10 (>6,000 ft) | 212°F |
| Whole tomatoes (Raw pack) | Quart | 45 | + 5 (1,000 to 6,000 ft), + 10 (>6,000 ft) | 212°F |
| Pickles (Sliced) | Pint | 10 | + 5 (1,000 to 6,000 ft), + 10 (>6,000 ft) | 212°F |
| Peaches (Halved) | Quart | 25 | + 5 (1,000 to 6,000 ft), + 10 (>6,000 ft) | 212°F |
| Applesauce | Pint/Quart | 20 | + 5 (1,000 to 6,000 ft), + 10 (>6,000 ft) | 212°F |

*U.S. Department of Agriculture. (2023).* Complete Guide to Home Canning. *Washington, DC: USDA.*

## PRESSURE CANNING

When pressure canning low-acid foods, your canner must maintain a temperature of 240°F through high-pressure steam in order to destroy bacteria like *Clostridium botulinum*. Note that you must account for your location's altitude, as it affects water's boiling point and pressure levels. For a comprehensive list of foods and their specific canning guidelines, refer to the National Center for Home Food Preservation.

**Dial-gauge pressure canner rule:** Increase pressure by 1 PSI for each 2,000 feet above sea level.

**Weighted-gauge pressure canner rule:** Use 15 PSI for all altitudes above 1,000 feet.

| FOOD TYPE | JAR SIZE | PROCESSING TIME (MINUTES) | DIAL-GAUGE PRESSURE (PSI) AT 0 TO 2,000 FEET | WEIGHTED-GAUGE PRESSURE (PSI) AT 0 TO 1,000 FEET | TEMPERATURE (°F) |
|---|---|---|---|---|---|
| Asparagus (Spears/Pieces) | Pints | 30 | 11 | 10 | 240°F |
| Asparagus (Spears/Pieces) | Quarts | 40 | 11 | 10 | 240°F |
| Green beans (Whole/Pieces) | Pints | 20 | 11 | 10 | 240°F |
| Green beans (Whole/Pieces) | Quarts | 25 | 11 | 10 | 240°F |
| Carrots (Sliced/Diced) | Pints | 25 | 11 | 10 | 240°F |
| Carrots (Sliced/Diced) | Quarts | 30 | 11 | 10 | 240°F |
| Corn (Whole Kernel) | Pints | 55 | 11 | 10 | 240°F |
| Corn (Whole Kernel) | Quarts | 85 | 11 | 10 | 240°F |
| Peas (Green/Shelled) | Pints | 40 | 11 | 10 | 240°F |
| Peas (Green/Shelled) | Quarts | 40 | 11 | 10 | 240°F |
| Potatoes (White/Cubed) | Pints | 35 | 11 | 10 | 240°F |
| Potatoes (White/Cubed) | Quarts | 40 | 11 | 10 | 240°F |
| Chicken or Rabbit | Pints | 75 | 11 | 10 | 240°F |
| Chicken or Rabbit | Quarts | 90 | 11 | 10 | 240°F |
| Beef stew | Quarts | 90 | 11 | 10 | 240°F |
| Vegetable soup | Quarts | 60 | 11 | 10 | 240°F |

*U.S. Department of Agriculture. (2023).* Complete Guide to Home Canning. *Washington, DC: USDA.*

NOTES

- **Dial-gauge pressure canners:** For altitudes above 2,000 feet, increase the pressure by 1 PSI for each additional 2,000 feet. For example, at 4,000 feet, use 13 PSI.

- **Weighted-gauge pressure canners:** At altitudes above 1,000 feet, use 15 PSI.

- **Processing times:** Always follow specified processing times to ensure the destruction of harmful bacteria.

- **Jar sizes:** Ensure you're using the correct jar size, as processing times can vary between pints and quarts.

## REGIONAL CONSIDERATIONS

Knowing your elevation is one of the simplest ways to ensure your canned goods are properly preserved and safe for long-term storage. Even a small elevation change can impact the safety of your canned goods, so it's essential to know your local altitude before starting a canning project. The following resources can help.

- Mountainous areas often require significant adjustments, especially above 2,000 feet.

- Lower altitudes (under 1,000 feet) typically don't need modifications.

- When in doubt, adjust conservatively—higher pressure or longer processing times are safer than underprocessing.

## MEASUREMENT CONVERSION CHARTS

### VOLUME CONVERSIONS

| MEASUREMENT | EQUIVALENT |
|---|---|
| 1 teaspoon | 5 milliliters |
| 1 tablespoon | 15 milliliters |
| ¼ cup | 60 milliliters |
| ⅓ cup | 79 milliliters |
| ½ cup | 120 milliliters |
| 1 cup | 240 milliliters |
| 1 quart | 960 ml or 4 cups |

### WEIGHT CONVERSIONS

| MEASUREMENT | EQUIVALENT |
|---|---|
| 1 ounce | 28 grams |
| 1 pound | 16 ounces |
| 1 kilogram | 2.2 pounds |

# INDEX

## A

acidity, role of, 24–25
allspice
  Ketchup, 120–121
almond extract
  Cherry Pie Filling, 196–197
Apple Butter, 68–69
Apple Chutney, 126–127
apple juice
  Apple Pie Filling, 194–195
apples
  Apple Butter, 68–69
  Apple Chutney, 126–127
  Apple Pie Filling, 194–195
  Caramelized Apple Chutney,
    127
  Chai-Spiced Apple Butter, 69
  Cranberry Apple Chutney,
    127
  Fruit Compote, 191
  Maple Apple Butter, 69
  Rum Apple Butter, 69
  Spiced Apple Chutney, 127
apricots, dried
  Fruity Chutney, 125
Asparagus, Pickled, 85

## B

bacon
  Pork and Beans, 176–177
Basic Chili, 178–179
Basic Creamed Corn, 107
basil
  Garden Vegetable Sauce,
    130–131
  Marinara Sauce, 116–117
  Meat Sauce, 136–137
  Meatballs in Sauce, 184–185
  Minestrone Soup, 152–153
  Pickled Bell Peppers, 82–83
  Pizza Sauce, 118–119
  Tomato Soup, 156–157
batch cooking, 169
batch processing, 17
bay leaves
  Beef Stock, 148–149
  Carrots, 100–101
  Chicken and Vegetable Stew,
    174–175
  Chicken Stock, 146–147
  Fish Stock, 144–145
  Mushroom Broth, 142–143
  Vegetable Broth, 140–141
BBQ Sauce, 122–123
beans and legumes

Basic Chili, 178–179
Beef and Root Vegetable
  Chili, 180–181
Black Bean Soup, 160–161
Lentil Soup, 162–163
Minestrone Soup, 152–153
Mixed Bean Soup, 164–165
Mixed Vegetables, 102–103
Pickled Three Bean Salad,
  170–171
Pork and Beans, 176–177
Split Pea Soup, 158–159
See also green beans
beef
  Basic Chili, 178–179
  Beef and Root Vegetable
    Chili, 180–181
  Beef Stew, 186–187
  Meat Sauce, 136–137
  Meatballs in Sauce, 184–185
  Sloppy Joe Filling, 182–183
beef bones
  Beef Stock, 148–149
Beef Stock
  Basic Chili, 178–179
  Beef and Root Vegetable
    Chili, 180–181
  Beef Stew, 186–187
  Meat Sauce, 136–137
  Meatballs in Sauce, 184–185
  Minestrone Soup, 152–153
  Mixed Bean Soup, 164–165
  recipe, 148–149
berries, mixed
  Berry Syrup, 190
  Honey-Sweetened Berry
    Jam, 74
  Low-Sugar Berry Preserves,
    72
  See also individual berry types
black beans
  Basic Chili, 178–179
  Black Bean Soup, 160–161
  Turkey Chili, 179
Blackberry Preserves, 63
Blueberry Jam, 60
botulism prevention, 12
Bread-and-Butter Pickles,
  90–91
brine, cloudy, 37
brine ratios, 79
broths. See stocks and broths
brown sugar
  Apple Butter, 68–69

Apple Chutney, 126–127
BBQ Sauce, 122–123
Ketchup, 120–121
Tomato Chutney, 124–125
bubble removers, 13
butters
  Apple Butter, 68–69
  Chai-Spiced Apple Butter, 69
  Mango Lime Butter, 77
  Maple Apple Butter, 69
  Rum Apple Butter, 69

## C

cabbage
  Minestrone Soup, 152–153
Canned Green Beans, 54–55
cannellini beans
  Minestrone Soup, 152–153
canning
  basics of, 23–24
  building confidence for, 11–12
  equipment for, 13–14
  myths about, 32, 42
  produce for, 14–17, 18
  setting up kitchen for, 12–13
  step-by-step instructions for,
    33–35, 49–52
  storage after, 19–21
  tips for, 37
  troubleshooting, 36–38, 53–54
canning funnels, 13
canning racks, 13
Caramelized Apple Chutney,
  127
cardamom
  Chai-Spiced Apple Butter, 69
carrots
  Beef and Root Vegetable
    Chili, 180–181
  Beef Stew, 186–187
  Beef Stock, 148–149
  Black Bean Soup, 160–161
  Carrots, 100–101
  Chicken and Vegetable Stew,
    174–175
  Chicken Soup, 166–167
  Chicken Stock, 146–147
  Fish Stock, 144–145
  Garden Vegetable Sauce,
    130–131
  Lentil Soup, 162–163
  Minestrone Soup, 152–153
  Mixed Bean Soup, 164–165
  Mixed Garden Pickle, 96
  Mixed Vegetable Pickle, 95

Mixed Vegetables, 102–103
Mushroom Broth, 142–143
Pickled Carrots, 84
Pickled Vegetable Medley,
  86–87, 172–173
Potato Soup, 154–155
Split Pea Soup, 158–159
Tomato Soup, 156–157
Vegetable Broth, 140–141
Vegetable Soup, 150–151
cauliflower
  Mixed Garden Pickle, 96
  Mixed Vegetable Pickle, 95
  Pickled Vegetable Medley,
    172–173
cayenne pepper
  Black Bean Soup, 160–161
  Ketchup, 120–121
  Lentil Soup, 162–163
  Sloppy Joe Filling, 182–183
  Spiced Apple Chutney, 127
  Spicy BBQ Sauce, 123
  Spicy Tomato Chutney, 125
celery
  Beef Stew, 186–187
  Beef Stock, 148–149
  Black Bean Soup, 160–161
  Chicken and Vegetable Stew,
    174–175
  Chicken Soup, 166–167
  Chicken Stock, 146–147
  Corn Relish, 98
  Fish Stock, 144–145
  Lentil Soup, 162–163
  Minestrone Soup, 152–153
  Mixed Bean Soup, 164–165
  Mixed Vegetable Pickle, 95
  Mushroom Broth, 142–143
  Potato Soup, 154–155
  Split Pea Soup, 158–159
  Tomato Soup, 156–157
  Vegetable Broth, 140–141
  Vegetable Soup, 150–151
celery seeds
  Bread-and-Butter Pickles,
    90–91
  Corn Relish, 98
  Mixed Vegetable Pickle, 95
  Pickled Three Bean Salad,
    170–171
  Pickled Vegetable Medley,
    86–87
  Sweet Relish, 97
  Zucchini Relish, 81

Chai-Spiced Apple Butter, 69
chard
    Mixed Greens, 110–111
cherries
    Cherry Pie Filling, 196–197
    Cherry Preserves, 64
chicken
    Chicken and Vegetable Stew, 174–175
    Chicken Soup, 166–167
Chicken Stock
    Black Bean Soup, 160–161
    Chicken and Vegetable Stew, 174–175
    Chicken Soup, 166–167
    Lentil Soup, 162–163
    Minestrone Soup, 152–153
    Mixed Bean Soup, 164–165
    Potato Soup, 154–155
    recipe, 146–147
    Split Pea Soup, 158–159
    Tomato Soup, 156–157
    Turkey Chili, 179
    Vegetable Soup, 150–151
chili powder
    Basic Chili, 178–179
    BBQ Sauce, 122–123
    Beef and Root Vegetable Chili, 180–181
    Pork and Beans, 176–177
    Spicy Pork and Beans, 177
    Tomato Chutney, 124–125
Chipotle Pepper Sauce, 133
chipotle powder
    Smoky and Sweet Chili, 179
chutneys
    Apple Chutney, 126–127
    Caramelized Apple Chutney, 127
    Cranberry Apple Chutney, 127
    Fruity Chutney, 125
    Herbed Chutney, 125
    Spiced Apple Chutney, 127
    Spicy Tomato Chutney, 125
    Tomato Chutney, 124–125
cilantro
    Herbed Chutney, 125
    Peach Salsa, 128–129
cinnamon
    Apple Butter, 68–69
    Apple Chutney, 126–127
    Apple Pie Filling, 194–195
    BBQ Sauce, 122–123
    Fruit Compote, 191
    Ketchup, 120–121
    Peach Pie Filling, 193
    Spiced Orange Marmalade, 71

Tomato Chutney, 124–125
Classic Dill Pickles, 88–89
cloudy brine, 37
cloves
    Apple Butter, 68–69
    Apple Chutney, 126–127
    BBQ Sauce, 122–123
    Ketchup, 120–121
    Spiced Orange Marmalade, 71
    Tomato Chutney, 124–125
cold plate test, 59
cooling, 30, 45
coriander
    Apple Chutney, 126–127
    Tomato Chutney, 124–125
corn
    Basic Creamed Corn, 107
    Corn, 106–107
    Corn Relish, 98
    Mixed Vegetables, 102–103
    Vegetable Soup, 150–151
cranberries, dried
    Apple Chutney, 126–127
    Cranberry Apple Chutney, 127
    Fruity Chutney, 125
cucumbers
    Bread-and-Butter Pickles, 90–91
    Classic Dill Pickles, 88–89
    Pickled Vegetable Medley, 86–87
    Sweet Pickled Gherkins, 92–93
    Sweet Relish, 97
cumin
    Basic Chili, 178–179
    BBQ Sauce, 122–123
    Beef and Root Vegetable Chili, 180–181
    Black Bean Soup, 160–161
    Lentil Soup, 162–163
    Mixed Pepper Sauce, 132–133
    Peach Salsa, 128–129
    Tomato Chutney, 124–125
curry powder
    Carrots, 100–101

**D**
desserts
    about, 189
    Apple Pie Filling, 194–195
    Berry Syrup, 190
    Cherry Pie Filling, 196–197
    Fruit Compote, 191
    Marmalade Pudding Topping, 192
dill

Carrots, 100–101
Classic Dill Pickles, 88–89
Pickled Asparagus, 85
Pickled Vegetable Medley, 86–87
dill seeds
    Classic Dill Pickles, 88–89
    Pickled Dilly Beans, 94
    Pickled Vegetable Medley, 86–87

**E**
equipment, 12–13

**F**
Fig and Orange Conserve, 76
First In, First Out (FIFO) rule, 20
Fish Stock, 144–145
floating food, 37
foam, reducing, 59
Fruit Compote, 191
Fruity Chutney, 125

**G**
Garden Vegetable Sauce, 130–131
garlic
    Apple Chutney, 126–127
    Basic Chili, 178–179
    BBQ Sauce, 122–123
    Black Bean Soup, 160–161
    Classic Dill Pickles, 88–89
    Garden Vegetable Sauce, 130–131
    Garlic-Infused Ketchup, 121
    Ketchup, 120–121
    Lentil Soup, 162–163
    Marinara Sauce, 116–117
    Meat Sauce, 136–137
    Meatballs in Sauce, 184–185
    Mixed Pepper Sauce, 132–133
    Mushroom Sauce, 134–135
    Peach Salsa, 128–129
    Pickled Asparagus, 85
    Pickled Bell Peppers, 82–83
    Pickled Carrots, 84
    Pickled Dilly Beans, 94
    Pickled Vegetable Medley, 86–87
    Pizza Sauce, 118–119
    Tomato Chutney, 124–125
    Tomato Soup, 156–157
garlic powder
    Meatballs in Sauce, 184–185
    Sloppy Joe Filling, 182–183
gauge testing, 44
gel setting, 31–32
ginger

Apple Chutney, 126–127
Chai-Spiced Apple Butter, 69
Marmalade Pudding Topping, 192
Tomato Chutney, 124–125
Gourmet Balsamic Ketchup
    Garlic-Infused Ketchup, 121
    recipe, 121
Grape Jelly, 67
green beans
    Canned Green Beans, 54–55
    Minestrone Soup, 152–153
    Mixed Garden Pickle, 96
    Mixed Vegetables, 102–103
    Pickled Dilly Beans, 94
    Pickled Three Bean Salad, 170–171
    Pickled Vegetable Medley, 86–87, 172–173
    Vegetable Soup, 150–151
Greens, Mixed, 110–111

**H**
habanero peppers
    Spicy Peach Salsa, 129
hardiness zones, 16
headspace tools, 13
Herbed Chutney, 125
Herb-Infused Sauce, 133
honey
    BBQ Sauce, 122–123
    Honey-Sweetened Berry Jam, 74
    Mixed Pepper Sauce, 132–133
    Peach Salsa, 128–129
    Sloppy Joe Filling, 182–183
hot packing, 29

**J**
jalapeños
    Peach Salsa, 128–129
    Pickled Vegetable Medley, 86–87
    Pineapple Jalapeño Jelly, 75
    Spicy Chili, 179
jams
    Blueberry Jam, 60
    Honey-Sweetened Berry Jam, 74
    Nectarine Jam, 73
    Plum Jam, 65
    Raspberry Jam, 66
    testing consistency for, 59
jar lifters, 13
jars
    breakage and, 38
    checking for spoilage, 20–21
    choosing, 13–14
    cooling, 30

preparation of, 30
sizes of, 14
storing after canning, 19–20
unsealed, 36
uses for, 14
jellies
Grape Jelly, 67
Pineapple Jalapeño Jelly, 75
testing consistency for, 59

**K**
kale
Mixed Greens, 110–111
Ketchup, 120–121
kidney beans
Basic Chili, 178–179
Beef and Root Vegetable
Chili, 180–181
Mixed Bean Soup, 164–165
Pickled Three Bean Salad,
170–171

**L**
labeling, 19
lemon juice
Apple Butter, 68–69
Apple Pie Filling, 194–195
Berry Syrup, 190
Blackberry Preserves, 63
Blueberry Jam, 60
Cherry Pie Filling, 196–197
Cherry Preserves, 64
Garden Vegetable Sauce,
130–131
Grape Jelly, 67
Honey-Sweetened Berry
Jam, 74
Low-Sugar Berry Preserves,
72
Marinara Sauce, 116–117
Nectarine Jam, 73
Peach Pie Filling, 193
Peach Preserves, 61
Pear Preserves, 62
Pickled Bell Peppers, 82–83
Pineapple Jalapeño Jelly, 75
Pizza Sauce, 118–119
Plum Jam, 65
Raspberry Jam, 66
Simple Strawberry Jam, 38–39
Whole Tomatoes, 80
lemons
Marmalade Pudding Topping,
192
Orange Marmalade, 70–71
Lentil Soup, 162–163
lids and bands, 13, 14
lime juice
Mango Lime Butter, 77
Mixed Pepper Sauce, 132–133

Peach Salsa, 128–129
liquid loss, 36
Low-Sugar Berry Preserves, 72

**M**
mangoes
Mango Lime Butter, 77
Tropical Peach Salsa, 129
maple syrup
BBQ Sauce, 122–123
Maple Apple Butter, 69
Smoky and Sweet Chili, 179
Marinara Sauce, 116–117
marmalades
Marmalade Pudding Topping,
192
Orange Marmalade, 70–71
Orange Rosemary Marma-
lade, 71
Spiced Orange Marmalade, 71
testing consistency for, 59
Whiskey Orange Marmalade,
71
mason jars, 13
meal planning, 169
meat, pressure-canning, 43–44
Meat Sauce, 136–137
Meatballs in Sauce, 184–185
menu planning, 169
Minestrone Soup, 152–153
mint
Herbed Chutney, 125
Mixed Bean Soup, 164–165
Mixed Braising Greens,
110–111
Mixed Garden Pickle, 96
Mixed Pepper Sauce, 132–133
Mixed Vegetable Pickle, 95
Mixed Vegetables, 102–103
moisture exposure, preventing,
19
molasses
BBQ Sauce, 122–123
Pork and Beans, 176–177
Sloppy Joe Filling, 182–183
Sweet and Smoky Beans, 177
mushrooms
Mushroom Broth, 142–143
Mushroom Sauce, 134–135
Mushrooms, 112–113
mustard powder
BBQ Sauce, 122–123
Ketchup, 120–121
Pork and Beans, 176–177
Sloppy Joe Filling, 182–183
mustard seeds
Apple Chutney, 126–127
Bread-and-Butter Pickles,
90–91

Carrots, 100–101
Classic Dill Pickles, 88–89
Corn Relish, 98
Mixed Vegetable Pickle, 95
Pickled Three Bean Salad,
170–171
Pickled Vegetable Medley,
86–87, 172–173
Sweet Relish, 97
Tomato Chutney, 124–125
Zucchini Relish, 81

**N**
navy beans
Mixed Bean Soup, 164–165
Pork and Beans, 176–177
Nectarine Jam, 73
nutmeg
Apple Butter, 68–69
Apple Pie Filling, 194–195
Carrots, 100–101

**O**
olive oil
Garden Vegetable Sauce,
130–131
Marinara Sauce, 116–117
Meat Sauce, 136–137
Meatballs in Sauce, 184–185
Mixed Pepper Sauce, 132–133
Mushroom Sauce, 134–135
Pickled Vegetable Medley,
172–173
Pizza Sauce, 118–119
one-jar meals
Basic Chili, 178–179
Beef and Root Vegetable
Chili, 180–181
Beef Stew, 186–187
Chicken and Vegetable Stew,
174–175
Meatballs in Sauce, 184–185
Pickled Three Bean Salad,
170–171
Pickled Vegetable Medley,
172–173
Pork and Beans, 176–177
Sloppy Joe Filling, 182–183
Smoky and Sweet Chili, 179
Spicy Chili, 179
Turkey Chili, 179
onion powder
Meatballs in Sauce, 184–185
onions
Apple Chutney, 126–127
Basic Chili, 178–179
BBQ Sauce, 122–123
Beef and Root Vegetable
Chili, 180–181
Beef Stew, 186–187

Beef Stock, 148–149
Black Bean Soup, 160–161
Bread-and-Butter Pickles,
90–91
Chicken and Vegetable Stew,
174–175
Chicken Soup, 166–167
Chicken Stock, 146–147
Fish Stock, 144–145
Garden Vegetable Sauce,
130–131
Ketchup, 120–121
Lentil Soup, 162–163
Marinara Sauce, 116–117
Meat Sauce, 136–137
Meatballs in Sauce, 184–185
Minestrone Soup, 152–153
Mixed Bean Soup, 164–165
Mixed Pepper Sauce, 132–133
Mushroom Broth, 142–143
Mushroom Sauce, 134–135
Peach Salsa, 128–129
Pickled Three Bean Salad,
170–171
Pickled Vegetable Medley,
86–87, 172–173
Pizza Sauce, 118–119
Potato Soup, 154–155
Sloppy Joe Filling, 182–183
Split Pea Soup, 158–159
Sweet Relish, 97
Tomato Chutney, 124–125
Tomato Soup, 156–157
Vegetable Broth, 140–141
Zucchini Relish, 81
orange juice/zest
Fig and Orange Conserve, 76
oranges
Marmalade Pudding Topping,
192
Orange Marmalade, 70–71
Orange Rosemary Marma-
lade, 71
Spiced Orange Marmalade, 71
Whiskey Orange Marmalade,
71
oregano
Beef and Root Vegetable
Chili, 180–181
Garden Vegetable Sauce,
130–131
Marinara Sauce, 116–117
Meat Sauce, 136–137
Meatballs in Sauce, 184–185
Minestrone Soup, 152–153
Mixed Bean Soup, 164–165
Pickled Bell Peppers, 82–83
Pickled Vegetable Medley,
172–173

Pizza Sauce, 118–119
Tomato Soup, 156–157
Vegetable Soup, 150–151

**P**
pantry, rotating, 169
paprika, smoked
  Basic Chili, 178–179
  BBQ Sauce, 122–123
  Beef and Root Vegetable
    Chili, 180–181
  Black Bean Soup, 160–161
  Lentil Soup, 162–163
  Meatballs in Sauce, 184–185
  Mixed Pepper Sauce, 132–133
  Pork and Beans, 176–177
  Sloppy Joe Filling, 182–183
  Smoky Ketchup, 121
  Smoky Peach Salsa, 129
  Tomato Chutney, 124–125
parsley/parsley stems
  Chicken and Vegetable Stew,
    174–175
  Chicken Soup, 166–167
  Meatballs in Sauce, 184–185
  Vegetable Broth, 140–141
parsnips
  Beef and Root Vegetable
    Chili, 180–181
peach juice
  Peach Pie Filling, 193
peaches
  Peach Pie Filling, 193
  Peach Preserves, 61
  Peach Salsa, 128–129
  Smoky Peach Salsa, 129
  Spicy Peach Salsa, 129
  Tropical Peach Salsa, 129
pears
  Fruit Compote, 191
  Pear Preserves, 62
peas
  Mixed Vegetables, 102–103
  Split Pea Soup, 158–159
pectin, 26
pepper, ground black
  Apple Chutney, 126–127
  Basic Chili, 178–179
  BBQ Sauce, 122–123
  Beef and Root Vegetable
    Chili, 180–181
  Beef Stew, 186–187
  Black Bean Soup, 160–161
  Chicken and Vegetable Stew,
    174–175
  Chicken Soup, 166–167
  Garden Vegetable Sauce,
    130–131

Ketchup, 120–121
Lentil Soup, 162–163
Meat Sauce, 136–137
Meatballs in Sauce, 184–185
Minestrone Soup, 152–153
Mixed Bean Soup, 164–165
Mixed Pepper Sauce, 132–133
Pizza Sauce, 118–119
Potato Soup, 154–155
Split Pea Soup, 158–159
Tomato Chutney, 124–125
Tomato Soup, 156–157
Vegetable Soup, 150–151
pepper flakes, crushed red
  Apple Chutney, 126–127
  Basic Chili, 178–179
  Classic Dill Pickles, 88–89
  Garden Vegetable Sauce,
    130–131
  Meat Sauce, 136–137
  Mixed Pepper Sauce, 132–133
  Pickled Asparagus, 85
  Pickled Bell Peppers, 82–83
  Pickled Dilly Beans, 94
  Pickled Vegetable Medley,
    86–87, 172–173
  Spicy Chili, 179
peppercorns
  Beef Stock, 148–149
  Carrots, 100–101
  Chicken Stock, 146–147
  Fish Stock, 144–145
  Mushroom Broth, 142–143
  Pickled Bell Peppers, 82–83
  Pickled Carrots, 84
  Vegetable Broth, 140–141
peppers, bell
  Black Bean Soup, 160–161
  Corn Relish, 98
  Garden Vegetable Sauce,
    130–131
  Mixed Pepper Sauce, 132–133
  Peach Salsa, 128–129
  Pickled Bell Peppers, 82–83
  Pickled Vegetable Medley,
    172–173
  Sloppy Joe Filling, 182–183
  Sweet Relish, 97
  Zucchini Relish, 81
peppers, chile
  Chipotle Pepper Sauce, 133
  Peach Salsa, 128–129
  Pickled Vegetable Medley,
    86–87
  Pineapple Jalapeño Jelly, 75
  Spicy Chili, 179
  Spicy Peach Salsa, 129
Pickled Asparagus, 85

Pickled Bell Peppers, 82–83
Pickled Carrots, 84
Pickled Dilly Beans, 94
Pickled Three Bean Salad,
  170–171
Pickled Vegetable Medley,
  86–87, 172–173
pickles
  Bread-and-Butter Pickles,
    90–91
  Classic Dill Pickles, 88–89
  Mixed Garden Pickle, 96
  Mixed Vegetable Pickle, 95
  Sweet Pickled Gherkins,
    92–93
pickling spices
  Mixed Garden Pickle, 96
  Sweet Pickled Gherkins,
    92–93
pineapples
  Pineapple Jalapeño Jelly, 75
  Tropical Peach Salsa, 129
pinto beans
  Mixed Bean Soup, 164–165
Pizza Sauce, 118–119
plums
  Fruit Compote, 191
  Plum Jam, 65
pork
  Meatballs in Sauce, 184–185
  Pork and Beans, 176–177
potatoes
  Beef Stew, 186–187
  Chicken and Vegetable Stew,
    174–175
  Chicken Soup, 166–167
  Lentil Soup, 162–163
  Minestrone Soup, 152–153
  Mixed Bean Soup, 164–165
  Potato Soup, 154–155
  Potatoes, 99
  Split Pea Soup, 158–159
  Vegetable Soup, 150–151
preserves
  Blackberry Preserves, 63
  Cherry Preserves, 64
  Peach Preserves, 61
  Pear Preserves, 62
pressure, monitoring, 45
pressure canners
  about, 13, 42
  calibrating and testing, 48
  choosing weight for, 46–47
  maintaining and cleaning,
    47–48
  storing, 48
pressure canning
  about, 41–42

foods not suitable for, 42–43
of meat, 43–44
myths about, 42
reference chart for, 198–199
safety for, 44–45
step-by-step instructions for,
  49–52
troubleshooting, 53–54
produce
  choosing, 14–15
  handling, 15–16
  seasonal, 16, 18
  storing, 15–16
Protein-Packed Sauce, 131
Pumpkin, 104–105
pumpkin, puréed, 42–43

**R**
raisins, golden
  Apple Chutney, 126–127
  Fruity Chutney, 125
  Tomato Chutney, 124–125
Raspberry Jam, 66
raw packing, 29
recipes, importance of following
  tested, 24, 45
relishes
  Corn Relish, 98
  Sweet Relish, 97
  Zucchini Relish, 81
Rich and Smoky Sauce, 137
Roasted Red Pepper Sauce, 131
rosemary
  Beef Stew, 186–187
  Orange Rosemary Marma-
    lade, 71
Rum Apple Butter, 69

**S**
salsas
  Peach Salsa, 128–129
  Smoky Peach Salsa, 129
  Spicy Peach Salsa, 129
  Tropical Peach Salsa, 129
salt, role of, 25–26
sauces
  BBQ Sauce, 122–123
  consistency guide for, 115
  Garden Vegetable Sauce,
    130–131
  Ketchup, 120–121
  Marinara Sauce, 116–117
  Meat Sauce, 136–137
  Mixed Pepper Sauce, 132–133
  Mushroom Sauce, 134–135
  Pizza Sauce, 118–119
  Smoky Hickory BBQ Sauce,
    123
  Spicy BBQ Sauce, 123

Sweet and Tangy BBQ Sauce, 123
shelf life, 20
Simple Strawberry Jam, 38–39
siphoning, 36
Sloppy Joe Filling, 182–183
Smoky and Sweet Chili, 179
Smoky Hickory BBQ Sauce, 123
Smoky Ketchup, 121
Smoky Peach Salsa, 129
soups and stews
  Beef Stew, 186–187
  Black Bean Soup, 160–161
  Chicken and Vegetable Stew, 174–175
  Chicken Soup, 166–167
  Lentil Soup, 162–163
  Minestrone Soup, 152–153
  Mixed Bean Soup, 164–165
  Potato Soup, 154–155
  Split Pea Soup, 158–159
  Tomato Soup, 156–157
  Vegetable Soup, 150–151
  See also stocks and broths
Spiced Orange Marmalade, 71
Spicy Apple Chutney, 127
Spicy BBQ Sauce, 123
Spicy Chili, 179, 181
Spicy Italian Sauce, 137
Spicy Peach Salsa, 129
Spicy Pork and Beans, 177
Spicy Tomato Chutney, 125
spinach
  Mixed Greens, 110–111
Split Pea Soup, 158–159
spoilage, signs of, 20–21
spoon test, 59
squash, summer, 42–43
Squash, Winter, 109
stocks and broths
  about, 139
  Beef Stock, 148–149
  Chicken Stock, 146–147
  cooking times for, 139
  Fish Stock, 144–145
  Mushroom Broth, 142–143
  selecting ingredients for, 139
  storing, 139
  straining, 139
  Vegetable Broth, 140–141
  See also soups and stews
storage, 19–21
Strawberry Jam, Simple, 38–39
sugar, role of, 25
summer squash, 42–43
Sweet and Smoky Beans, 177

Sweet and Smoky Meat Sauce, 137
Sweet and Tangy BBQ Sauce, 123
Sweet Pickled Gherkins, 92–93
sweet potatoes
  Beef and Root Vegetable Chili, 180–181
  Sweet Potatoes, 108
Sweet Relish, 97
Sweeter Sauce, 133

T
temperature control, 30–31
temperature test, 59
theme nights, 169
thickness, adjusting, 115
thyme
  Beef Stew, 186–187
  Beef Stock, 148–149
  Chicken and Vegetable Stew, 174–175
  Chicken Soup, 166–167
  Garden Vegetable Sauce, 130–131
  Meat Sauce, 136–137
  Mixed Bean Soup, 164–165
  Mushroom Broth, 142–143
  Mushroom Sauce, 134–135
  Potato Soup, 154–155
  Split Pea Soup, 158–159
  Vegetable Soup, 150–151
time and temperature control, 30–31
timers, 13
timing, 17
tomato paste
  BBQ Sauce, 122–123
  Garden Vegetable Sauce, 130–131
  Ketchup, 120–121
  Meat Sauce, 136–137
  Sloppy Joe Filling, 182–183
tomato sauce
  Pork and Beans, 176–177
  Sloppy Joe Filling, 182–183
tomatoes
  Basic Chili, 178–179
  BBQ Sauce, 122–123
  Beef and Root Vegetable Chili, 180–181
  Garden Vegetable Sauce, 130–131
  Ketchup, 120–121
  Marinara Sauce, 116–117
  Meat Sauce, 136–137
  Meatballs in Sauce, 184–185
  Minestrone Soup, 152–153

Mixed Bean Soup, 164–165
Mixed Garden Pickle, 96
Mixed Pepper Sauce, 132–133
Mushroom Sauce, 134–135
Pizza Sauce, 118–119
Tomato Chutney, 124–125
Tomato Soup, 156–157
Vegetable Soup, 150–151
Whole Tomatoes, 80
Tropical Peach Salsa, 129
Turkey Chili, 179
turmeric
  Bread-and-Butter Pickles, 90–91
  Corn Relish, 98
  Sweet Pickled Gherkins, 92–93
  Sweet Relish, 97
  Zucchini Relish, 81

V
vanilla extract
  Fruit Compote, 191
Vegetable Broth
  Black Bean Soup, 160–161
  Lentil Soup, 162–163
  Potato Soup, 154–155
  recipe, 140–141
  Split Pea Soup, 158–159
  Tomato Soup, 156–157
  Vegetable Soup, 150–151
vegetables
  crispness and, 79
  selecting, 79
  See also individual vegetables
Vegetarian Beans, 177
venting, 44–45
vinegar, apple cider
  Apple Chutney, 126–127
  BBQ Sauce, 122–123
  Beef Stock, 148–149
  Bread-and-Butter Pickles, 90–91
  Chicken Stock, 146–147
  Fish Stock, 144–145
  Ketchup, 120–121
  Minestrone Soup, 152–153
  Mixed Pepper Sauce, 132–133
  Mushroom Broth, 142–143
  Peach Salsa, 128–129
  Pickled Bell Peppers, 82–83
  Pork and Beans, 176–177
  Sloppy Joe Filling, 182–183
  Tomato Chutney, 124–125
  Tomato Soup, 156–157
  Vegetable Broth, 140–141
  Vegetable Soup, 150–151
vinegar, balsamic

Garlic-Infused Ketchup, 121
Sweet and Tangy BBQ Sauce, 123
vinegar, pickling
  Bread-and-Butter Pickles, 90–91
  Classic Dill Pickles, 88–89
  Corn Relish, 98
  Mixed Garden Pickle, 96
  Mixed Vegetable Pickle, 95
  Pickled Asparagus, 85
  Pickled Carrots, 84
  Pickled Dilly Beans, 94
  Pickled Three Bean Salad, 170–171
  Pickled Vegetable Medley, 86–87, 172–173
  Sweet Pickled Gherkins, 92–93
  Sweet Relish, 97
  Zucchini Relish, 81

W
water, impact of, 27
water bath canners, 13
water bath canning
  myths about, 32
  reference chart for, 198
  step-by-step instructions for, 33–35
  tips for, 37
  troubleshooting, 36–38
water levels, 30
wax beans
  Pickled Three Bean Salad, 170–171
Whiskey Orange Marmalade, 71
Whole Tomatoes, 80
wine, red
  Meat Sauce, 136–137
  Mushroom Sauce, 134–135
  Winter Squash, 109
Worcestershire sauce
  BBQ Sauce, 122–123
  Meat Sauce, 136–137
  Pork and Beans, 176–177
  Sloppy Joe Filling, 182–183
  Tomato Chutney, 124–125

Z
zucchini
  Garden Vegetable Sauce, 130–131
  Minestrone Soup, 152–153
  Vegetable Soup, 150–151
  Zucchini Relish, 81

# BIBLIOGRAPHY

Appert, Nicolas. *The Art of Preserving All Kinds of Animal and Vegetable Substances for Several Years. A Work Published by Order of the French Minister of the Interior, on the Report of the Board of Arts and Manufactures.* London: Black, Parry and Kingsbury, 1811. Retrieved from https://www.loc.gov/item/48039359/

*Ball Blue Book of Canning and Preserving Recipes.* Cookbooks, Promotional materials, Recipes. Szathmary Recipe Pamphlets. Retrieved from https://digital.lib.uiowa.edu/node/12454

Encyclopedia of Life Support Systems: Principles of Food Preservation. Developed under the Auspices of UNESCO, EOLSS Publishers, Paris, France. n.d. Retrieved from https://www.eolss.net

Fallon, Sally. *Nourishing Traditions: The Cookbook that Challenges Politically Correct Nutrition and the Diet Dictocrats.* White Plains, MD: NewTrends Publishing, 2001.

Karel, M., and Lund, D. *Physical Principles of Food Preservation: Revised and Expanded* (2nd ed.). Boca Raton: CRC Press, 2003. Retrieved from https://doi.org/10.1201/9780203911792

National Center for Home Food Preservation. Historical Records on Food Preservation. Retrieved from https://nchfp.uga.edu/

U.S. Department of Agriculture. (2023). *Complete Guide to Home Canning.* Washington, DC: USDA.

University of Minnesota Extension. Food Safety and Preservation: A Home Canner's Guide. Retrieved from https://extension.umn.edu/

# ACKNOWLEDGMENTS

This book would not have been possible without the support, inspiration, and guidance of many incredible individuals and organizations.

To Jenny Croghan at HarperCollins, thank you for throwing a shot in the dark and reaching out to me that fine November day. Writing this book is something I have dreamed about since I was a child.

To my family and friends, thank you for being my enthusiastic taste testers and for cheering me on during every stage of this journey. Your encouragement has been invaluable, and your feedback has made every recipe better.

I extend my deepest gratitude to the mentors and teachers who have shared their knowledge of traditional food preservation. Your wisdom has inspired me to carry forward these timeless practices and adapt them for today's kitchens.

A special thank-you to the Weston A. Price Foundation and its cofounder, Sally Fallon, for their dedication to promoting nourishing, time-honored cooking methods. Your resources have been a beacon of inspiration throughout this project.

Finally, to my readers, thank you for your curiosity and passion for preserving. It is my hope that this book serves as a guide and companion in your journey to capture the beauty of seasonal flavors and preserve them for generations to come.

With deep gratitude,
MOLLY BRAVO

Author image by John Valenti, javelinteacreative.com

## ABOUT THE AUTHOR

Molly Bravo is the founder of Wylder Space, a movement dedicated to reclaiming traditional food preparation and intentional living. With nearly two decades as a chef, educator, and advocate for the Real Food Movement, Molly empowers families to reconnect with their kitchens and roots through simple, wholesome cooking.

Molly's passion for local, seasonal ingredients and timeless practices like canning and fermenting inspires others to embrace the magic of home-cooked meals. Through Wylder Space, Molly makes even the most intimidating techniques approachable, helping people rediscover the joy of real food and meaningful connections.

Learn more at **www.wylderspace.com**

# ABOUT CIDER MILL PRESS
# BOOK PUBLISHERS

Good ideas ripen with time. From seed to harvest, Cider Mill Press brings fine reading, information, and entertainment together between the covers of its creatively crafted books. Our Cider Mill bears fruit twice a year, publishing a new crop of titles each spring and fall.

"Where Good Books Are Ready for Press"
501 Nelson Place
Nashville, Tennessee 37214, USA

cidermillpress.com